I0057538

BITCOIN AGE
Copyright © 2025 by Nik Bhatia
All rights reserved.

All rights reserved. No part of this publication may be reproduced,
distributed, or transmitted in any form or by any means, including
photocopying, recording, or other electronic or mechanical methods,
without the prior written permission of the publisher, except in the
case of brief quotations embodied in critical reviews and certain
other noncommercial uses permitted by copyright law.

ISBN   978-1-7361105-7-7

Cover and interior designed by Anton Khodakovsky

PRINTED IN THE UNITED STATES OF AMERICA

BITCOIN

AGE

NIK BHATIA

For Chandni and Ria

CHAPTER 1

MIND TRICKS

G ENTLY LANDING HIS BRUISED SPACESHIP ON THE scorching sands of a remote desert planet, a Jedi warrior readies his crew for a search. Together, they set out looking for a hyperdrive generator to fix their aircraft, weaving through a town of narrow alleyways lined with every variety of merchant.

The Jedi's focus is singular—he must find a mechanic. He arrives at a dimly lit workshop, where a large insect-looking creature emerges from the shadows, fluttering his wings as he surveys the newcomers. The mechanic offers a blunt greeting.

"What do you want?" he rasps as his eyes gleam with interest.

"I need parts for a J-Type 327 Nubian," the Jedi warrior responds.

The mechanic claims to have the generator in his inventory and assures the warrior that his spaceship can be fixed.

"How do you plan to pay for all of this?" the hovering creature inquires, already counting his income from the extensive cost of repair.

"I have 20,000 Republic credits," the Jedi declares.

For a moment, the mechanic simply stares. Then, with a slow, deliberate shake of his head, his wings abuzz with agitation, he scoffs. "Republic credits? Republic credits are no good out here. I need something *more real*," he demands, rubbing his fingers together, desiring a payment with more tangibility.

A heavy silence ensued. The Jedi understands his predicament—in this lawless corner of the galaxy, not all currency holds weight.

Trapped and without any other form of money at his disposal, he resorts to part of his craft: mind control. "Credits will do fine," the warrior proclaims, waving his hands near the mechanic's head in a practiced and methodical way.

"No, they will not," refuses the mechanic.

"Credits will do fine," the warrior repeats and waves again, unsure why his magic powers aren't working on the flying creature.

At this point, the mechanic loses his patience and accurately accuses his customer, "You think you're some sort of Jedi waving your hands at me? Mind tricks won't work on me! *Only money*."

Only money. Didn't the warrior offer the mechanic money? The Jedi would say yes, but not from the perspective of those on this desert planet; a faraway government's credits do not suffice as money, as the mechanic is unwilling to accept them as payment for his services. Without means to buy the part, the Jedi enters a wager to win his spaceship's repair.

The fictional multiplanetary exchange between warrior and mechanic from this poignant scene in *Star Wars: Episode I – The Phantom Menace* perfectly encapsulates this book's quest: to examine why billions of people exchange their precious time and labor for credits in the absence of a better money, and to explain how bitcoin fills that void.

Money is defined by something that is accepted as payment, while currency is defined by what circulates, oftentimes by legal decree, within a certain place. Why does the mechanic refuse the Galactic currency, which is accepted on multiple planets? Because this winged local lives in a corner of the galaxy that doesn't recognize the warrior's foreign currency. Credits from a distant planet, to him, fall short as money because he doesn't believe in their value.

The word credit comes from the Latin word *credere*, which means to believe—for as long as credit has existed, people tolerate it because they *believe* it to be money. There are two major problems, however, in believing in credit. First, it doesn't hold value over time—it's money, but only *temporarily*. Second, its uneven creation and distribution leave most people feeling like the chips are stacked against them.

We can demonstrate this inequity by comparing incomes with housing prices. In 1971, the median income in the United States was $9,000, while the median home cost $25,000—this meant that Americans could buy a home with about two and a half years of earnings. Today, the average earner brings home $80,000, but the average house costs $420,000, which is over five years' worth of income. Wages gradually rise under the credit system, but unfortunately for the everyday worker, the cost of living increases even more because the power to create credit is in the hands of the select few, disadvantaging billions of people who lack commensurate access.

Owning bitcoin has proven a marvelous solution over the past decade, allowing people to save in a money that makes prices go *down*. When the US commodities regulator legalized bitcoin futures trading in 2016, which we argue commenced the *Bitcoin Age*, the price of a median American home cost over ฿500 (500 bitcoin). Despite homes doubling in price by 2025, the median American home now costs less than ฿5. As this trend continues, people are improving their lives by saving in a money with *permanence*. As the price of bitcoin rises from $100,000 today to $1 million and beyond, one bitcoin will purchase multiple homes.

Bitcoin was created as a *technology response* to bank bailouts, currency debasement, and concentrated power of those who create credit. Therefore, we cannot understand bitcoin without comprehending the colossal size and reach of the very credit system it is designed to combat. This book outlines credit-money's journey and rise to global dominance and why it is unlikely to be displaced. It then chronicles bitcoin's spectacular ascent and how bitcoin presents the most innovative alternative to credit-money our species has ever encountered. Ultimately, we dissect why prices will always rise when measured in dollars but will continue to fall when measured in bitcoin.

The *Bitcoin Age* is defined by a tale of two parallel worlds—a dollar-fueled machine of institutions with the power to create unlimited amounts of money, and a revolutionary technology that was designed to help the common man survive such a rigged system. With the invention of bitcoin, humankind has finally discovered a solution to disproportionally rising prices: universally accessible digital money with a *limited* supply, controlled by no one. Bitcoin, which lets people transact without government currencies or bank accounts, utilizes software freely available to anybody with a smartphone and the internet, resulting in a tool that, if harnessed correctly, frees people from the shackles of credit. Bitcoin is the arrival of *better money*.

For thousands of years, humans equated money with treasure—gold, silver, or anything considered precious. Over time, governments and banks issued credits, capitalizing on a human desire for convenience. These credits—currency and deposits—carried value because they were backed by something very important: *hidden treasure*. However, that is no longer the case—the mind trick played on the world is that today's money isn't backed by anything. Furthermore, banks have convinced us that the benefits of dollar banking to society warrant central bank public backstops. Bailouts administered by these central banks enable unchecked banking misbehavior and guarantee the system's perpetual expansion. Dollars will continue to furnish the global economy, as the extension of credit underpins trade, investment, and securities markets, but people must finally recognize the power banks have over their choice in money. If time is our most precious resource, we should be exchanging it for something equally valuable, not something fleeting that can be so easily diluted.

Finally, people are emerging with an unprecedented ability to protect themselves by securing real money—bitcoin's limited supply helps people combat disparities caused by the global banking dollar. Credit-money isn't going anywhere, but as more people discover bitcoin's advantages as a superior store of value, bitcoin will emerge as the new global reserve asset. It will compete with over $400 trillion in real estate and cash assets for capital and become the world's preferred wealth measurement tool and storage vehicle. An economic network of a billion bitcoin users disrupts the global banking complex, and it also offers mesmerizing implications for the peaceful collaboration of humankind and empowers the individual like never before. This book will bring you up to speed on the transformation underway and explain why the *Bitcoin Age* is just getting started.

CHAPTER 2

THE CLANDESTINE
DUCK HUNT

A TYPICAL AMERICAN HOME USES 50,000 NAILS AND 25,000 screws in its construction. If building the house manually, it would take 15 seconds to hammer each nail and 30 seconds to apply each screw with a screwdriver, translating into 500 hours of labor consumed. By introducing nail guns and power drills, however, builders could accomplish the same task in only 100 hours, reducing the framing of a house from several months to a few weeks. Ideally, better technology and less labor should cause the cost of constructing the house to fall.

This same principle applies to almost everything in an economy. Businesses are always looking for ways to lower costs through efficiency and deliver the lowest possible price to the customer. As they gain customers, enterprises can scale production and cut costs even more. Think of a carpenter that makes wooden furniture. At first, he buys lumber at retail prices, uses manual tools, and spends time on new designs for a small customer base. After gaining experience and customers, he can cut time and costs by reapplying designs, buying lumber in bulk at lower wholesale prices, and purchasing automatic machinery that reduces the time to construct each item. If his business grows even more, he can start up a factory which will, over time, lower unit costs once again.

If businesses are always becoming more efficient, improving quality, and lowering prices for their customers, why instead, in the real world, do prices generally rise? The short answer is that we live in a credit system that *counteracts* the force of falling prices. Let's start by explaining what a *credit system* is.

A credit system begins when a worker accepts currency that *promises* to pay gold instead of the gold coin itself. At this point, he has accepted credit-money, whether for convenience or a blind trust in the currency issuer. Next, he deposits said currency in a bank, which is where the trouble of credit-money begins. Without any say in the process, his bank awards a $100 million loan to its corporate client to build a factory, and new deposits are suddenly created—those deposits do not come from somebody else but are instead fresh credits that the bank creates from thin air. The loan might generate some economic benefits, such as the company hiring a construction crew, but that has little direct impact on the worker whose deposits were just diluted because of the loan approval. That is how a credit system operates: credits circulate as currency, and most of them are created out of nothing. Then, the company buys available steel from local suppliers and depletes their inventories. Finally, steel producers feel empowered to increase prices because the company that just received a loan is a large source of new demand materially affecting the steel market.

Credit gets created when a borrower and a lender come together in a mindset of confidence. Both parties lead to the creation of new credit-money in a loan: the borrower wishes to consume now instead of later, and the lender can achieve profit if a creditworthy borrower pays back the loan plus interest. Home purchases, business investment such as the building of factories and hiring of workers, and even consumer purchases are largely financed with *new credit-money*. The cycle continues as confidence persists, new money continues to flood the economy, and demand for goods, services, and labor goes up—this machine is the primary driver of rising prices, also called price inflation.

Then, at a certain point, human nature takes over, and confidence turns into fear. Prices and debt rise beyond affordability at current incomes. Spending slows down to accommodate the larger debt service, and borrowers are no longer willing to take on new debt. Banks then create less money—a drop in new borrowing corresponds to a drop in lending. Without new money being created at the same pace, demand and prices start to fall. This is called a *credit cycle*.

It is at this point of the credit cycle that banks begin to panic. When prices fall, so do incomes. Anybody who has taken out a loan that sees incomes fall now faces a harder time paying back debt. To make matters worse, falling prices motivate people to *save*, instead of spend. More saving exacerbates the problem of a slowing economy, and those that have taken on too much debt start to default. Defaults cause the credit-money system to contract—money literally disappears from the system. This leads to more reduced spending, recessions, and as defaults add up, bank failures. Hopefully we can now understand why banks must avoid any hint of falling prices—they must prevent too much contraction, because profitable lending is what keeps them in business. Banks are therefore *reliant* on a combination of system-wide credit expansion and rising prices.

Credit expansion, while contributing to inflation, also helps the credit system pay for itself. Borrowed money must be paid back with interest, but if borrowed money is newly created, where will the money required to pay the interest come from? Here's an example to illustrate why expanding the system lifts all boats and makes it easier for borrowers to pay back interest and lenders to avoid defaulting borrowers. Banks lend $20 million to the businesses across a brand-new town, creating $20 million of new deposits within the local economy. The businesses hire people and produce goods, and the $20 million circulates throughout the town. If the businesses borrowed that money for one year at 5% interest, they would owe $1 million in interest expense for a total repayment of $21 million. If only $20 million in deposits exist within the entire economy, how will each business be able to afford repayment of principal plus interest? As money circulates throughout the economy, there will be some businesses that win, and others that lose, causing some loans to default. But if the bank lends another $3 million across the economy during the year, there is theoretically enough new credit circulating to help *all* original borrowers pay off their principal and make their interest payments. In that spirit, banks are motivated to increase the total amount of credit in the system year after year to give their customers the best chance of repayment. On the flipside, defaults shrink the quantity of credit, so defaults must be avoided by the financial system because they reduce the total money available for debt service and repayment.

The credit cycle ebbing and flowing causes prices to fluctuate, but banks prevent contractions from occurring as much as possible. Over the course of the past century, banks have implemented a credit system that protects themselves from the threat of falling prices, creating a world of haves and have-nots with their selective invitations to receive the flow of credit. Banks tower over our society because, for the entirety of the human species, it has been impossible to transfer value across time and space without trusting an intermediary. But they have abused this power, engineering a society that has institutionalized inflation. In that world, the cost of living for most people is rising faster than incomes: those who work in industries connected to the banking system benefit from increased incomes and can outpace a rising cost of living, but large disparities exist between those who are able to keep up and others who feel like they are falling further behind. Creating what others tirelessly work for punishes savers and gives bankers and their largest clients an outsized influence over society. Those closest to the money tap are limited only by their proficiency in capturing the flow, while those further away from it are unlikely to catch even a sparing droplet because they weren't invited inside the room.

In *six steps*, this book explains the origins of today's omnipotent credit system of disproportionate rising prices that cause people to either fall behind or chase risky investments just to keep pace with credit expansion. These episodes in financial history transformed a credit system anchored by money—gold—into a self-governed credit-money system, wherein banks create their own rules. The first three steps are featured in this chapter—forming a central bank to prevent sudden and unnecessary bank failures, establishing deposit insurance to increase confidence in credit-money, and banning people from holding gold as money within the United States. Our *first step* toward credit-system dominance begins when banks used a financial crisis in 1907 to convince the public a *central bank* was needed to bolster belief in the credit system.

* * *

Famous figures from American history shaped experiments with two early versions of a central bank—Alexander Hamilton, pictured on the $10 bill, led the charge to create the First Bank of the United States, while Andrew Jackson, who is pictured on the $20 bill, killed the Second Bank of the United States by vociferously fighting back against banker influence over the national currency. In the wake of these two expiring 20-year central banking charters, the US entered an era of *free banking* in 1837 wherein gold, silver, Treasury certificates, and banknotes all circulated as money. In the disorganized monetary mayhem, over 7,000 types of banknotes circulated throughout the nation, most of them used only locally and with little real-world utility. Overall, free banking laws resulted in both catastrophic failures and reasonably well-functioning banks.

In 1863 and 1864, the National Banking Acts finally brought some order to the United States monetary system, establishing an official system for national banks and a national currency—leaving behind the chaos of 7,000 banknotes with varying quality. State-based banks either closed or received national charters that came with the exclusive permission to create US dollars. One of the first national charters went to Citibank in 1865 after it relinquished its New York state charter. Founded in 1812 as a de facto successor to the First Bank of the United States, City Bank of New York was better known by its cable address, the eight-letter telegraph code CITIBANK.[1] The bank ascended to global superpower in 1891 after it was taken over by a pair of American business giants.

James Stillman's father, Charles, was one of the largest landowners in Texas, was connected to the banking industry, and built a successful enterprise that spanned all the way to Mexico. Charles sent James to study in England as a young boy, groomed him as the future of the family business, and

---

1   *Phillip Zweig, Wriston.*

tied him into the banking world by arranging his marriage to the daughter of Citibank's president. James continued in his father's line, bolstering the Stillman family's banking network and constructing railroads throughout Texas and Mexico. His associate in the railroad business was William Rockefeller, cofounder of Standard Oil with his older brother and American tycoon John D. Rockefeller.

William Rockefeller and James Stillman had a close relationship—Stillman's two daughters both went on to marry sons of Rockefeller. Together, they saw an opportunity to grab hold of Citibank in 1891, with the Rockefeller family recognizing the bank's potential usefulness in financing its global expansion. The family understood that with Citibank as a financing arm, Standard Oil increased its chances of outmaneuvering its competition. At the turn of the 20th century, Citibank and its rival J.P. Morgan sat atop the American financial system in lieu of a central bank, which hadn't existed in the US since the 1830s.

The crisis that pushed the US to implement a central bank was the Panic of 1907. After New York's third-largest trust company failed, J.P. Morgan hosted meetings in his personal library, physically locking the doors on the country's banking elite until they devised a plan to rescue key institutions and avoid a catastrophe.

Panics begin with bank runs—depositors ask for their money back when they fear the bank doesn't have it on hand. A bank run can be thought of as the action of claiming hidden treasure, converting credits to money; it is a crisis of confidence wherein the credits rapidly become worthless. The existence of a central bank can help prevent or mitigate bank runs because consumers assume their banks will survive turmoil by using the shared backstop. US Senator Nelson Aldrich, who was father-in-law to John D. Rockefeller and heavily connected to banking interests, took up the renewed charge for a central bank in the legislative branch after the financial crisis, but he couldn't get any momentum until Henry Davison got involved.

Starting out as an errand boy at a bank as a teenager, Davison rose quickly on Wall Street. He became one of the youngest partners ever at J.P. Morgan and helped to coordinate the response to the Panic of 1907, earning his reputation as Wall Street's premier financial crisis manager. Aldrich's agenda floundered without a specific action plan that satisfied all parties, while some political opposition built without swift action by the bankers. Davison took the wheel from the Senator and carefully manipulated the necessary players in his new approach.

The Davison-Aldrich scheme was clandestine at best and nefarious at worst. Bankers believed that as they produce a societal benefit by lending to productive participants in the economy, government policies should be in place to help them during a crisis. Davison and his fellow bankers wanted a central bank for themselves. The first stage of this plan was to arrange a secret meeting, knowing its true purpose would elicit public dissent. Next, they would create a federal institution that protected private interests—a redistribution justified by its supposed greater good. Finally, the plan hinged on ultimately seizing control of the United States national currency, unified under the National Banking Acts of 1863 and 1864.

Jekyll Island, distinguished as one of the world's most exclusive social clubs, served as the host to this highly secretive gathering. William Rockefeller and J.P. Morgan, two of only a few dozen club members, almost certainly arranged the venue, though neither participated in the private gathering itself.

A surreptitious arrangement with hints of an Agatha Christie plot, Davison instructed everyone to use either shortened first names or nicknames, board the specific rail car *Aldrich Private Car #40* without acknowledging one another on the train ride from New Jersey to Georgia and maintain the cover story that the sole purpose of the expedition to Jekyll Island was merely a duck hunt. In reality, the group was heading south to draw up plans for the ultimate club— a central bank to act as a reserve fund and bailout mechanism, leveraging the American government for authority. The group worked day and night for over a week, and despite the first documentation of the meeting appearing four years later, it would take over 20 years before any of the collaborators publicly admitted to having attended the meeting.

Davison and Aldrich were joined by a few key players, including another young banker within J.P. Morgan's inner circle named Benjamin Strong, German financier Paul Warburg, and Citibank executive Frank Vanderlip. Strong, like Davison, was a Wall Street star from a young age, earning control of Bankers Trust from Morgan at only 39 years old. Warburg was widely considered one of the world's experts on global banking and wrote abundantly about the need for a US central bank, while Vanderlip garnered the attention of James Stillman as a highly skilled banker after managing the $200 million US Treasury bond raise to fund the Spanish-American War. Vanderlip, Stillman's right hand at Citibank, wrote the final draft of the plan for the nation's central banking system after meetings on Jekyll Island between the country's preeminent bankers concluded and inserted a section that allowed US banks to establish overseas branches, an important regulation with an impact later in our story.[2]

In 1913, the duck hunters got their central bank and protective backstop when President Woodrow Wilson signed the Federal Reserve Act into law, creating a hybrid entity of Federal Reserve Banks, owned and controlled by the banks themselves, *and* the Federal Reserve Board, answerable to Congress and the American people. Almost two decades later, Warburg characterized the Jekyll Island meeting as a covert operation:

> *Though eighteen years have gone by, I do not feel free to give a description of this most interesting conference concerning which Senator Aldrich pledged all participants to secrecy.*[3]

---

2   Zweig, Wriston.

3   Griffin, G. Edward. *The Creature from Jekyll Island.*

Later, Frank Vanderlip also echoed Warburg's sentiment on the stealthiness of the entire affair:

I do not feel it is any exaggeration to speak of our secret expedition to Jekyll Island as the occasion of the actual conception of what eventually became the Federal Reserve system. Discovery, we knew, simply must not happen, or else all our time and effort would be wasted. If it were to be exposed publicly that our particular group had got together and written a banking bill, that bill would have no [chance.]

By creating the Federal Reserve system (the Fed), the United States finally centralized its currency under one entity, shrouded beneath a veil of secrecy by the country's top bankers. Congress maintained oversight, but banks had absorbed the dollar into their own sphere, with a federally legislated backstop for their system of credits to ensure that any contraction would quickly be remedied by a government-associated institution.

The Fed's creation was only the first step taken by banks to ensure the credit-money system's survival and dominance. A United States central bank would build public confidence that the banking system could rely on a central institution for emergency support, but banks needed much more than just a backstop.

*   *   *

The 1929 United States stock market crash had cascaded into a depression by 1931, and a lack of international financial coordination to address the crisis caused it to spread globally. In the spring of that year, the Rothschild-controlled Austrian bank Credit Anstalt failed to secure enough government support during a liquidity crisis. After the bank collapsed despite international assistance, the global financial crisis intensified. Nobody believed that countries would be able to honor credits promising to pay gold, as the quantity of credits far outstripped each country's gold reserve. Germany and Hungary ended their currencies' gold convertibility weeks later, and on September 19, 1931, the UK government shattered the global gold-exchange standard by suspending convertibility of the British pound. It then drastically devalued the currency.

One by one, each of the 47 countries on the gold-exchange standard abandoned it after the UK's surrender. The Fed's gold coverage—its ratio of gold to currency in circulation—dropped to the point that the average holder of dollars also feared devaluation and rushed to convert dollars to gold coin. In 1933, President Franklin D. Roosevelt ordered a series of actions to slash gold's grip on the financial system: he made it illegal for Americans to save in gold, forced them to sell their gold to the Fed at $20.67 per ounce, and then immediately devalued the dollar by adjusting the gold price up by 69% to $35. The *second step* was complete: destroy the link between money and credit by making it illegal to save in gold. That essentially mandated the use of bank deposits instead of allowing the citizenry a choice between money and credit.

The system's overhaul continued with a legal protection for depositors. After 9,000 bank failures between 1929 and 1933, the United States Congress passed the Banking Act of 1933, with the cornerstone of this legislation a federal guarantee on deposits—a move that forever changed banking and the entire human interaction with credit-money. In the face of thousands of bank failures despite a central bank backstop, Americans had become afraid of holding bank credits. In the *third step* toward credit-system dominance, deposit insurance was instituted as part of the Federal Deposit Insurance Corporation (FDIC), placing a safety umbrella over American deposit banking. Credits, for the first time ever, were *guaranteed* by the government.

Deposit insurance simultaneously began an era without quality checks: no longer would a depositor prudently measure if a bank was being responsible since any failure was now insured. This generally increased the trust in deposits because people felt like these credits no longer had risk. Banks had yearned for a mechanism to prevent deposit flight and avoid dislocations in their funding during contractions in the credit cycle—and by removing the uncertainty of bank failure, deposit insurance provided just that.

The creation of the FDIC was well-intended. If savers picked the wrong bank, one that happened to fail, their deposits would be insured by the federal government. Consumer protection is a crucial feature of a public utility, and the FDIC presented further evidence that US dollar deposit banking was part of that utility and viewed as a common right to be protected by law. Deposit insurance also calms the customer's mind when choosing a bank—if the government is to cover any individual bank's losses, discernment isn't as needed.[4] One financial historian, who wrote a book on the rise of Citibank, pointedly identified the FDIC as the transformative force for banking to move "from a carnival to a sedate public utility."

While deposit insurance helped assuage fears about the American banking system, an even more important component of the Banking Act to our story called *Regulation Q* influenced money to flee the country. Regulation Q capped deposit rates that banks could offer to customers, hoping to limit destabilizing competition between banks. If banks were barred from offering higher interest rates than their competitors, deposit flight would decline as people felt less compelled to chase the best rate in town. Ramifications of this reactionary regulation—its failure only visible in hindsight—drove dollar activity abroad.

---

4   *Henry Kaufman, Interest Rates.*

CHAPTER 3

INTERGALACTIC COMPUTER NETWORK

THE WORD 'PROTOCOL' COMES FROM THE GREEK WORD *prōtokollon*, made of up *prōtos*, meaning 'first,' and *kolla*, meaning 'glue.' The term originally described the first sheet in a papyrus roll: the *prōtokollon* would include the date, author, manufacturer, and other details to understand the contents within. It later became the French word *protocole*, taking on the meaning of a set of diplomatic etiquette rules. Over time, 'protocol' has become the word we use to describe software rules followed by everyone in a network. Network protocols give us the policies and procedures of a computer environment and help us build compatible tools for online interaction.

One of the first versions of a communications protocol, in which rules are set for two parties to communicate, was Morse code. It's a language transmitted with a code, and as long as both sides of the conversation can translate the code into words, the protocol works as intended and people can send messages across electric telegraphs. For Morse code to work, the language must be set in stone to establish uniformity in electronic messaging—or made into a *protocol*. Technological networks, from Morse code to the bitcoin protocol, cannot function unless everybody is following the same set of rules. Bitcoin's story as an entirely computer-based money begins with the first vision of a computer network.

* * *

In the early 19th century, the most effective way to communicate over long distances was by visual signals. In 1791, Claude Chappe developed an optical relay system that used flashing lights, which could be decoded through a structured communications protocol. This was similar to Morse code, but with lights, towers, and mirrors instead of the long and short beeps of the telegraph. The towers were spaced out, but at the speed of light, messages could be transferred extremely quickly even if each relay took time. Before Chappe's system, the fastest way to send a message was by horse. After his innovation, however, his team was able to transmit a short message a distance of 10 miles in four minutes—a speed of approximately 150 miles per hour.

Optical relays significantly shifted the collective mentality toward quicker communication, and innovation accelerated. In yet another technological leap, Joseph Henry invented the first electric telegraph in 1831, proving that information could be transmitted virtually. Many had developed similar ideas, but with the invention of Morse code and

$30,000 in United States government support for the necessary telecommunications infrastructure, the first 40-mile telegraphic message was sent from Washington, D.C., to Baltimore in 1844, a moment that shifted human consciousness to feel information at its fingertips.[5] By 1860, the United States had 50,000 miles of telegraph lines, laid alongside a newly expanded network of railway tracks. Railway stations established themselves as the communication hubs of their day, with one of the first commercial data transmissions between stations being stock prices. More importantly for the financial system, telegraphic communication worked perfectly for the transfer of bank balances which opened the possibility of a system not bound by anything physical such as metal or paper.

New York and Mississippi Valley Printing Telegraph Company was one of several dozen blossoming telegraph companies across the US in the early 1850s. In 1857, the company and five others merged to form Western Union—four years later, the first transcontinental telegraph message was sent from San Francisco to Washington, D.C. Electronic communication encompassed the nation, paving the way for money to enter the telegraphic arena.

Western Union created the first private money-order product, which let a person send credits to another via telegraph, anywhere in the country and faster than ever. Western Union emulated ancient Medici bookkeeping transfer methods, wherein bankers in different parts of the world helped

---

5   Tom Wheeler, *From Gutenberg to Google.*

transfer value via accounting and messengers instead of physical transfer of cash and coin. Telegraphic money orders showed banks how to capitalize on more modern communication networks for financial services. It takes one bank to create money and two to circulate it: as a result, the telegraph empowered swift monetary expansion due to the ease of electronic communication between hundreds or thousands of banks.

Telegraph lines eventually became telephone lines, followed by teleprinters—machines connected to each other via existing voice phone lines that would print out messages, like an early form of email. Teleprinter exchanges, or telex for short, became the preferred method for bank wires after American Telephone and Telegraph Company (AT&T) brought telex technology from Germany to the United States in 1954. Shortly thereafter, a joint venture between Western Union and the British Post Office led to the first transatlantic telephone cable, wired phone call, and telex message between the two continents—credits could now electronically circumnavigate the globe. The ease of messaging increased the confidence of credit-issuing authorities to probe the boundaries of dollar creation.

* * *

Psychoacoustics is the science of how human beings perceive sound—the field of study possesses a fascinating connection to the internet's creation. When Alexander Graham Bell invented the telephone in 1875, the Bell Telephone Company and its subsidiary AT&T set out to monopolize the new form of communication in the United States. Successful in its efforts, AT&T kept a stronghold on long-distance telephone calls: for 70 years it held a monopoly over all long-distance phone lines, in part thanks to the creation of Bell Labs.

Harvey Fletcher served as the first Director of Physical Research at Bell Labs and is considered the father of psychoacoustics, inventing the modern electronic hearing aid and demonstrating how three sound channels can be recorded using separate microphones and produce playback that creates staging—which he demonstrated at Carnegie Hall in 1933. Fletcher developed an acoustics theory in 1940 which explains how the inner ear processes frequencies, and his work underpins all speech recognition and audio compression technology today. It served as the foundation for the work of the internet's earliest shepherd, J.C.R. Licklider.

Joseph Carl Robnett Licklider had a remarkable ability to see many years into the future. As the third director of the US Department of Defense's Advanced Research Projects Agency (ARPA), Licklider—known as "Lick" to friends and colleagues—was part of a pioneering contingent determined to push computer networking to new heights. His ideas were truly novel, and his paper "Man-Computer Symbiosis" made him the perfect person to orchestrate the internet's founding.

Licklider triple majored in physics, math, and psychology as an undergraduate at Washington University in St. Louis in 1937 and earned doctorates in psychoacoustics and psychology from the University of Rochester in 1942. Immediately after finishing his studies, he went to work at Harvard's Psycho-Acoustic Laboratory, studying how humans process complex sounds and theorizing on information processing. He then moved over to MIT's Acoustics Laboratory, where he started brainstorming a future of interaction between humans and computers, before ultimately finding his true calling as the internet's first visionary.

In 1948, acoustician Leo Beranek co-founded Bolt, Beranek, and Newman (BBN), one of the most influential independent research labs in American history, to consult on architectural acoustics for buildings such as the United Nations Assembly Hall in New York and the Sydney Opera House in Australia. The company later transitioned its efforts to computing, and Beranek hired Licklider in 1957 to explore new horizons. There, Licklider published "Man-Computer Symbiosis" and outlined the future of computing:

> *The hope is that, in not too many years, human brains and computing machines will be coupled together very tightly, and that the resulting partnership will think as no human brain has ever thought.*[6]

Telex dominated communication at the time, but the US military was keen on investigating the potential of computers and, more importantly, how to connect them to each other over long distances. ARPA was founded in 1958 by President

---

6   J.C.R. Licklider, "Man-Computer Symbiosis."

Dwight D. Eisenhower as a direct response to the Soviet satellite Sputnik orbiting the Earth in 1957. The agency initially focused on the space race but quickly yielded that role to NASA. ARPA then switched its mission to improving ballistic missile technology, but once again lost that assignment to another section of the Defense Department. Looking for its next purpose during the Cold War, the agency's leadership created the Information Processing Techniques Office entirely for Licklider to accelerate the Defense Department's command over computers.

To carry out his vision, Licklider needed the help of the country's brightest minds. Immediately, he reached out to the nation's top research institutions, funded new labs and entire departments, and fired up the academic-governmental machine required to begin networking computers together.[7] Thanks to his university funding initiatives, computer scientists secured grants to acquire computing equipment, advancing their capacity to build such an indispensable network. His vision was immortalized by the memo he sent around to his ARPA colleagues in 1963, in which he conceptualized the internet and called for a protocol:

Consider the situation in which several different centers are netted together, each center being highly individualistic and having its own special language and its own special way of doing things... It seems to me to be important... to develop a capability for integrated network operation.

---

7   *Katie Hafner and Matthew Lyon, Where Wizards Stay Up Late.*

Licklider understood that coordination was mandatory and assigned the work to researchers across MIT, Stanford, University of California—Berkeley, and the University of California—Los Angeles (UCLA). He also contracted with private institutions such as his former employer BBN, assembling a team that was known as "Lick's priesthood"— scientists around America ready to build the internet's first skeleton. Licklider called it the *Intergalactic Computer Network*.

CHAPTER 4

THE GLOBAL BANKING DOLLAR

SSUANCE OF UNITED STATES DOLLARS TODAY, BIZARRELY, is not controlled by the United States government. One might assume, rightfully, that the dollar is a purely American phenomenon, regulated by a combination of the US government and the Federal Reserve, but that's not the case. One of the primary reasons for this peculiar conundrum emerges from a story of City of London bankers who figured out how to create dollars without United States permission, or even knowledge. Expansion of the credit system—and simultaneous dilution of the dollar—accelerated after European bankers seized an opportunity to profit from the dollar credit-money system in the 1950s, transforming the dollar into a global banking currency of the powerful and well connected. The *fourth step* toward institutionalizing our credit system was the obfuscation of the dollar's true parent by London bankers. Instead of fighting this takeover, United States policymakers accepted that a *global banking dollar* was the US dollar's new form.

As World War II came to a close, countries were ready for a new currency regime after the crumbling of the international gold standard. With Europe's capital essentially destroyed—buildings, factories, and infrastructure leveled to the ground—a new global financing currency evolved out of the necessity to rebuild. US dollars replaced British pounds in global trade financing by greater margins each passing year, and the system's new design now centered around dollar credit creation. The Bretton Woods Conference of 1944 created the International Monetary Fund, World Bank, and crowned the US dollar as the world's monetary fulcrum—currencies around the world would become redeemable for dollars. Pounds and francs were not to be priced in specific amounts of gold, but at a fixed exchange rate versus the US dollar. The dollar would maintain a fixed price versus gold at $35 per ounce, with the agreement's intent being to bring the world under a stable exchange rate regime. Dollars became the global unit of account, its financial measuring stick. Instead of stability, the world experienced chaos and banks opened up a new frontier as a result of the Bretton Woods agreement.

George Bolton identified that frontier and seized the opportunity long before others did. As a board member of the Bank of England and the UK's central man at the newly formed International Monetary Fund, nobody had a better vantage of the British pound's role in global currencies than Bolton—the currency had long lost its dominance to the dollar by 1957, which left British bankers in a precarious position. Bolton was regarded as the country's foremost expert on foreign exchange, and he understood that for London to continue its legacy as the international financial center, it would have to reinvent itself, outsmart the bankers in New York, and think beyond the bounds of gold. In 1957, he left the Bank of England to become the chairman of the Bank of London and South America (BOLSA), a British overseas bank with most of its dealings in Brazil and Argentina, resolute to save the City of London.

A UK currency crisis that same year forced the country to restrict the issuance of British credits outside its borders. The new regulation had an unintended consequence: British banks turned to the best available alternative—the US dollar. Dollar lending in the UK started when companies that earned dollars from exports to the US deposited their earnings in European banks. Banks took these foreign-domiciled dollars as a funding source for lending activity in the City of London— British banks started lending these dollars back out, and the overseas dollar market took on an entire life of its own. Bolton had just taken over as Chairman of BOLSA and promptly ditched British pounds as his preferred currency—he grew BOLSA's dollar deposits from $3 million in 1957 to almost $300 million in 1960.[8] The interesting quirk about Bolton's bank was its British overseas status, meaning BOLSA fell outside the scope of UK oversight. Consider George Bolton's predicament, or indeed, stroke of luck: his bank wasn't regulated by the UK because it operated offshore and in dollars, and it

---

8   Gary Burn, "The State."

wasn't regulated by the US because it wasn't a US bank and had no operations within the country—despite accounting in, accepting deposits in, and lending US dollars. Bolton had stumbled upon something unique that defined and shaped the next monetary era: *unregulated money.*

* * *

Prior to George Bolton's creativity, US dollars were already circulating throughout Europe. As the United States gained economic power and industrial prowess during the early 20th century, dollars flowed around the planet as Americans purchased goods, services, and commodities worldwide. Every time dollars were sent abroad to make purchases, US currency would either return—if foreigners purchased American exports, stocks, and bonds—or it would simply stay overseas. In 1950, China had amassed some dollar reserves from global trade but needed somewhere to keep them; the Chinese Communist Party hired the Hungarian Central Bank as an acting agent to deposit $5 million on its behalf into BCEN, a French bank with strong Soviet ties and origins.[9] China's reasons were geopolitical: during World War II, the United States and the Federal Reserve Bank of New York had sequestered gold belonging to Yugoslavia under war protocols, leaving a scar in the minds of any actor fearful of the political ramifications of holding US dollar deposits in New York. Reports are that even prior to the Chinese government,

---

9   Burn, *"The State."*

Soviet nations, heedful of the Yugoslav incident, deposited dollars with BCEN in the late 1940s. During this Cold War period, European-domiciled dollar deposits took on a geopolitical importance in the financial positioning between the United States and the Soviet Union.

Political ideology had seeped into the banking system, forcing nations to choose where to store the new global reserve currency. With the US dollar featured in most global transactions, holding dollars became strategically important for all nations, even the ones who were scared to bank with an American bank. Overseas dollar banking, in its early days, often went through BCEN—dollars sent to BCEN over the telex network used the bank's telex address EUROBANK-BCEN, which became Eurobank dollars, and then more plainly, Eurodollars.[10] The name stuck. A *Eurodollar* became the descriptor for a dollar *outside the United States banking system.*

Let's briefly outline how the Eurodollar works relative to deposits held in US banks. Somebody in California writes a check to somebody in New York. The person in New York deposits the check, and the New York bank calls the California bank for funds to settle. Both banks have an account at the Federal Reserve which they naturally call *reserves.* Reserves are part of the monetary base, or *high-powered money,* which is money issued by the central bank. Banks leverage high-powered money and other forms of financial collateral to lend new credit-money into existence—also called the money multiplier effect.

---

10   *Josh Younger, "Eurodollars and Petrodollars"*

The California bank instructs a transfer of reserves to the New York bank, and their customers' transaction is complete. If, on the other hand, a BCEN client in Paris writes a dollar check to a Barclays client in London, how does BCEN send dollars to Barclays to settle the transaction? The answer is a book entry—in simple terms, BCEN says "I owe you" to Barclays and issues a credit, and Barclays marks the BCEN credit as an asset. That BCEN credit is called a *Eurodollar deposit*—it's a dollar promise from a bank that isn't located in the United States to another bank that's also located outside the US. Eurodollar banks operate *without a central bank*, meaning there is no high-powered money serving as a settlement tool nor as a basis for multiplying money.

It's not that BCEN doesn't have any capital, collateral, or dollars in reserve—Eurodollar banks often own a combination of dollar cash, dollars on deposit with banks in the United States, and US Treasuries to leverage in credit creation. But it doesn't have central bank reserves, so when it grows money supply by issuing a Eurodollar deposit to Barclays, it has grown the global supply of dollars with no capacity restriction placed on it by any American authority. When Barclays accepts the Eurodollar credit from BCEN as an asset, we now have a separate dollar system that can grow independently of American banking activity and without a regulated boundary on its multiplier. That's exactly what started to develop—a London offshore dollar universe that US authorities did not sanction, create, or explicitly endorse. When confronted with this globalization of the US dollar, the country decided to allow its progress, primarily because Eurodollar activity extended US political and financial power.

*   *   *

Away from Cold War politics, London's practice of attracting and deploying dollars outside of the United States was motivated by profit, and the legacy of early Eurodollar banking still dominates today's modern financial landscape. Operating today as HSBC, Midland Bank was a Eurodollar pioneer. The bank solicited dollars in 1955 for a potentially profitable trade. Due to Regulation Q in the US that capped deposit rates offered by US banks, Midland attracted dollar deposits from those seeking a higher interest rate than could be achieved in New York. The bank invested those dollars into British pounds, which offered higher interest rates than dollars did at the time. Midland had generated a very low-risk profit utilizing Eurodollars and arbitraging interest rates across currencies and showed its peers how to play this new game of offshore, unregulated dollar banking.[11] Regulation Q was an attempt to help US banks by preventing deposit flight, but the opposite occurred—New York banks suffered a severe disadvantage to City of London banks that could offer higher interest rates, especially when market-based rates were on the rise, as they were during the period.

British banks custodied US currency in vaults and carried deposit balances with New York banks, but they didn't abide by a standardized protocol for dollar issuance, such as a

---

11   Catherine Schenk, "Eurodollar Market."

reserve ratio, like US banks did. George Bolton inspired other London banks to use the dollar more liberally than banks in the United States and bring dollar banking activity to the UK even though the currency carried the name of a distant neighbor. During this *fourth step*, London cemented its position as the international financial center despite the British pound permanently falling from grace as the world's financing currency—an opportunistic subversion of American currency sovereignty. Dollar issuance was no longer controlled by any United States institution, public or private.

In 1957, deposits at Citibank were stagnating. Regulation Q, an economic recession, and restrictions on customer acquisition—New York banks could only serve New York residents—all constrained the bank's ability to generate profit. But something changed that reinjected life into the plagued bank. One of the foreign exchange officers at Citibank heard through the grapevine that another US bank had accepted deposits in London and paid an interest rate higher than what was allowed in the United States under Regulation Q. This seemingly innocent jurisdictional anomaly was far from insignificant. American banks had found a way around one of the most oppressive regulations of the past 25 years, unleashing a rapid transformation in the global dollar system. Citibank's leaders knew they needed the Eurodollar market to survive. Citibank and other American banks were on the global banking dollar scene as early as 1958, starting or revitalizing branches in the City of London.[12] In 1961, Citibank developed an instrument

---

12   *Zweig, Wriston.*

to raise deposits explicitly in the offshore market, bolstering the overseas dollar system and demonstrating that US policymakers had no control over it. By 1964, Chase Manhattan, Citibank, and Bank of America were all present in London, relying on dollar deposits to help fund their operations.[13]

* * *

Blurred lines between money and credit empowered bankers in the 1950s. By the end of the decade, the Federal Reserve was fully aware that American banks, inspired by the UK-based Midland Bank in particular, had set up shop in the City of London to exploit the Eurodollar market. Still restricted by Regulation Q, American banks could not leave themselves out of the open market for deposits, so they went to the UK. In doing so, American banks legitimized the dollar's break from US control.

The new global banking dollar system required an upgrade in communications protocol. In 1960, Citibank, Bank of America, Chase Manhattan, Barclays, Lloyds, and Midland Bank led an effort to standardize messaging between banks for settlement of wires around the world—the precursor to today's SWIFT system. The creativity of British overseas banks, geopolitical incentives to avoid New York banking, City of London profiteering, and the survival instincts of American banks all contributed to the rise of the Eurodollar system, and the Fed had finally taken notice.

---

13 *Gianni Toniolo, Central Bank Cooperation.*

Not to be caught off guard, the American central bank sent Alan Holmes and Fred Klopstock, two of its senior officials, to Europe to investigate what they called Continental dollars before the Eurodollar moniker caught on. Holmes and Klopstock concluded that the new system wasn't necessarily an explicit problem because it increased the size of the dollar network. Even if it was a problem, it wasn't one in the hands of Fed officials. A key finding was that American banks themselves were already active in the market:

> *Overseas branches of United States banks have become depositories of very sizable amounts of Continental dollars, running into several hundreds of millions of dollars. They have used the market as a means to recapture some of the time deposits that had escaped, or were about to escape their head offices, because of the interest rate ceiling on such deposits under Regulation Q.* [14]

One conclusion from the Fed's visit was that New York was losing the international lending battle to London, which paradoxically caused a greater internationalization of the dollar, a bargain that the Fed understood all the way back in 1960 and chose to accept. The global banking dollar ironically reinforced the US dollar's network effect—when Americans import goods and those dollars are held in reserve abroad, there is more potential demand for dollar assets, such as US Treasuries, corporate bonds, and mortgages of American

---

14   *Alan Holmes and Fred Klopstock, "Dollar Deposits."*

homeowners. This makes borrowing easier for the United States, its companies, and its citizens. Ultimately, Holmes and Klopstock determined that this European-based dollar system contributed to global dollar adoption, and the Fed should find no reason to stop what was already entrenched:

[The] fact remains that the Continental dollar market has given birth to a new relatively high-yielding and now firmly entrenched and widely used outlet for the short-term investment of dollar funds. In this sense the dollar has become more useful, and banks operating in this market will probably tend to hold on to dollar assets for more extended periods than they would in the absence of the market.

In only a handful of years, the Eurodollar system of unregulated dollar banking in Europe had exploded. Growth aside, the very nature of the dollar itself had changed— American policy existed only in the distance. At a May 1962 meeting of the International Institute of Banking, one Swiss banker described Eurodollars as money that had escaped US authorities and were now under *no one's control.*[15] In 1962, the formation of the Eurobond market was the Eurodollar's first triumph. Just as Eurodollar deposits replicated dollar deposits in American banks, the Eurobond market replicated the US bond market outside of any US regulation. Now, companies and countries anywhere in the world could borrow

---

15 *Seung Woo Kim, "Knowledge."*

dollars in London that might never have graced the balance sheet of a US bank instead of relying on their local bond markets, and holders of Eurodollar deposits could reinvest them in dollar-based investments offering interest rates comparable to or even better than US-based securities.[16]

Telex machines empowered the system's growth, as credits took the form of *messages* transmitted over cables. The power to create and transmit dollars via the telex network gave Eurodollar banks outside the United States—including American banks with overseas branches—immense and incomparable power. Declassified CIA documents show that Singapore was chosen as Asia's Eurodollar market hub in 1969 by Citibank and Chase Manhattan because of its strong connection to the global telex network.[17] Creation and circulation of dollars was never easier for this unregulated cartel of offshore banks.

---

16 *Jeremy Green, "Anglo-American."*

17 *CIA, "The Asia-Dollar Market."*

CHAPTER 5

INFORMATION AGE

BATTLING LOS ANGELES TRAFFIC WHILE DRIVING FROM work to graduate school, Paul Baran was struggling to balance his two commitments. Born in then-Poland, today part of Belarus, he moved to the United States as an electrical engineering student to attend UCLA, attaining a master's degree in engineering studying computers and transistors. Baran decided to continue his doctoral study while working at the RAND Corporation, a military-centric think tank that worked closely with the Air Force on air missile defense systems.

One late afternoon, as Baran drove from the RAND offices in Santa Monica to the UCLA campus in Westwood, he arrived only to face an immense challenge in finding a parking spot. Already frustrated with the lack of time due to an intense doctoral workload and a time-consuming research job, Baran decided to take it as a sign from above that his doctoral pursuit had ended, "At that instant I concluded that it was God's will that I should discontinue school. Why else would He have found it necessary to fill up all the parking lots at that exact instant?" This parking mishap led to a groundbreaking networking discovery that helped lay the foundation for the internet.

While he studied defense communications as a full-time researcher at RAND, the Cold War raged on, and nuclear war was on everybody's mind, including Paul Baran's. Military communications relied on extremely fast transmission, which was subject to disruption if key relay points were taken down by adversaries. In 1960, the fastest message relays available depended on the ancient technology of telephone switching—a monopoly held at the time by AT&T. To call somebody long distance, an operator would have to physically switch the inputs and outputs of wired connections along the way, sometimes several times, to allow one cross-country connection.

Baran found a military reliant on centralized manual operators unacceptably slow, archaic, and subject to attack. He understood that if an enemy bombed a single hub connecting one part of the country to the next, the disruption could entirely cripple the US military's ability to communicate—a threat of unfathomable proportion. As the solution, Baran came up with the idea of distributed networking and specifically *packet switching*, in which information would be broken up into little pieces and sent across varying and diversified routes only to reach their destination and reassemble, delivering the full message using multiple paths simultaneously.

The idea, which underpinned the internet's eventual architecture, bewildered the folks at AT&T, whose monopoly over long-distance telephone switching would not be ceded to an unproven theory. AT&T engineers told Baran that he had no concept of how telecommunications worked, quickly dismissing the notion of such a build-out. Despite RAND's support and the endorsement of AT&T's own Bell Labs, Baran's idea went nowhere thanks to the incumbents at AT&T. Baran later said about the telephone monopoly:

Their attitude was that they knew everything and nobody outside the Bell System knew anything. And somebody from the outside couldn't possibly understand or appreciate the complexity of the system.[18]

Instead of convincing AT&T, which he knew was a lost cause, Baran decided to take matters into his own hands:

After I heard the melodic refrain of 'bullshit' often enough, I was motivated to go away and write a series of detailed memoranda papers, to show, for example, that algorithms were possible that allowed a short message to contain all the information it needed to find its own way through the network.

He spent four years and authored 11 volumes to detail why packet switching was the future, leaving the breadcrumbs for whichever government agency was ready to take on the challenge of reinventing communication. Baran's diatribe was

---

18   *Hafner and Lyon, Wizards.*

left to marinate until somebody who didn't require AT&T's blessing dusted it off.[19]

*   *   *

A veteran of the US Navy, Bob Taylor joined ARPA in 1965 after working on computer graphics research at both MIT and NASA. Taylor brought a strong history of public service to his role at ARPA, assuming the post previously held by J.C.R. Licklider. Upon his arrival, he felt frustrated with the inability to connect the computing power of his new computer in Santa Monica to MIT's or UC Berkeley's. Each research department wanted more computing power, but instead of buying room-sized computers and shipping them across the country, why not connect the universities' computers via a network so that information and computing power could be shared?

Bob Taylor presented the idea to the agency's director who immediately granted the project a $1 million budget to begin connecting various ARPA-contracted research centers to one another. The director later admitted that he had been waiting for such a proposal, Licklider, years before, had mentally prepared ARPA for the arrival of an Intergalactic Computer Network. To enact his plan, Taylor needed a telecommunications expert and identified Larry Roberts, a PhD in electrical engineering who was working on air defense at MIT's Lincoln Labs. Roberts was initially hesitant to join, but

---

19   *Andrew Russell, Open Standards.*

because the government funded 51% of Lincoln Labs, Taylor exercised political sway to bring Roberts aboard.

Larry Roberts was already well-versed in Licklider's writings and was well positioned to help Taylor and ARPA realize the vision of a world where interconnected computers could seamlessly communicate. Roberts was known as a tireless worker—he had already sketched out what the network might look like before arriving at the Pentagon on his first day. One of Roberts' best friends and Las Vegas blackjack card-counting running mate, Larry Kleinrock, got the first phone call. A UCLA professor and fellow electrical engineer and doctorate in computer science from MIT, Kleinrock was selected by Roberts to establish the network's measurement center and receive the first node in the new ARPA network, or *ARPANET*.

In 1967, two years after the ARPANET proposal, a meeting was held in Ann Arbor, Michigan, to assemble the country's research centers—a meeting of minds to explore how to build out the new network. At that conference, Wes Clark, a physicist also working at Lincoln Labs, brought forward an idea to connect small computers—the earliest version of internet routers—to form the network instead of connecting university computers to each other. Larger computers, each with their own languages, would be difficult to network, but if each large computer connected to a routing node, these small, interconnected nodes could process all communication. Today, this can be thought of as a WiFi router—the router handles the connection to the internet so that your device itself doesn't have to.

The Ann Arbor conference also identified distributed networking and packet switching as starting points, citing Paul Baran's work that had been shut down by AT&T. Packet switching made sense for ARPANET's architecture because it would break up large data before reassembling it, allowing the network to use telephone lines that had limits in their transmitting capacity. By the end of the meeting, momentum for the network was underway. In 1968, BBN beat out IBM, Raytheon, other competitors for the ARPA contract to build the router-like interface message processor (IMP), the machine envisioned by Wes Clark. Upon the prototype's completion, Roberts delivered IMP 1 to his Vegas partner Kleinrock at UCLA.

When building these early routers, BBN experienced deadline crunches, but the company delivered on its promise to the Defense Department. Most importantly, the routers were expected to work. When IMP 1 arrived at UCLA, it was the size of a refrigerator, weighed almost a thousand pounds, and had four steel eyebolts on top of the machine so that cranes or helicopters could lift it. At UCLA, though, IMP 1 fit inside the elevator despite some doubts on whether it would fit, and the machine was taken to the third floor where it found its home.

The following month, a crew at Stanford Research Institute (SRI) received IMP 2, readying the scene for ARPANET's first transmission. Finally, the two computers in Southern California and Northern California could attempt communication. On the UCLA campus in the fall of 1969, Leonard Kleinrock's small research team gathered around their computer for the historic moment. Three computer science researchers were about to attempt something envisioned only by the era's advanced technological dreamers: communication between computers, built by different manufacturers, 300 miles apart. Kleinrock described their goal: "All we wanted to do ... was to send a simple login capability from UCLA to SRI. We just wanted to login to the SRI machine from UCLA."

Bill Duvall, a researcher at SRI, awaited the message from Los Angeles while on the phone with his UCLA counterparts for a live narration of the attempt. "We were hooked up with a telephone headset, and we were talking to each other," Duvall described. Charley Kline, a member of Kleinrock's team at UCLA, started typing the word *login*.

"The first thing I typed was an L," recounted Kline. Duvall told Kline the letter L had appeared on his screen. "I typed the O, and he got the O," Kline continued. Duvall saw the letters "LO" on his screen at SRI, at which point the computer crashed, but not before sending shivers down his spine. The transmission, despite the abrupt curtailment, had *worked*.[20]

With ARPANET's first test complete, the network was ready to grow—IMP 3 was sent to UC Santa Barbara and IMP 4 to the University of Utah. After the original four, ARPANET was expanding by one node per month. As demand for data transmission expanded as a testament to the network's early success, the previously skeptical AT&T was forced to install new telephone lines linking Los Angeles to Boston

---

20 *Guy Raz, "Communication Revolution."*

(over 3,000 miles) and Utah to Boston (over 2,000 miles) to improve connectivity. As the network of nodes grew, universities, military think tanks, and the Defense Department all took an active interest in the network's technicalities and sought to finalize a protocol to establish standardized rules crucial for its build-out.

Even though the internet started from United States government funding and military-trained engineers, its technical components were built by young computer science students and researchers at California universities who believed in transparent and open collaboration. One of them was UCLA student Steve Crocker, who documented every protocol discussion and dispute on the way to consensus. The first meeting's minutes, or Request for Comments, were published by Crocker in 1969, setting a fundamental precedent of open documentation, discussion, and healthy dispute on internet protocol development that carries through to bitcoin today. A participant in the early meetings praised the accessibility of the culture around building internet protocols:

When you read [Request for Comments] 1, you walked away from it with a sense of 'Oh, this is a club that I can play in too'.[21]

In 1971, the group produced the Network Control Protocol, the first standardized rule set for computers to communicate with each other over telephone lines.

---

21   *Hafner and Lyon, Wizards.*

*   *   *

The next step in protocol evolution was to bring the concept of distributed packet routing to the world, which the Network Control Protocol did not do. Early development resulted in a closed network, but the internet's dreamers envisioned the entire world having access. To use the ARPANET, users required a government-issued router, and once they joined the network, only the data on the network was accessible—the open internet didn't yet exist. Other networks were popping up over radio or satellite communication, and computer users were starved for a way to communicate outside of their walled gardens. The Network Control Protocol served the ARPANET well but could not function on a more global basis. Bob Kahn and Vint Cerf invented a solution.

Kahn worked for BBN and directly contributed to the IMP design while at the firm, while Cerf studied for his doctorate at UCLA. They were two of the earliest users of the ARPANET at UCLA, and soon they came together to work on what ultimately became the rules of today's internet. The two computer scientists delivered a paper outlining a transmission-control protocol (TCP) which explained how messages could be sent and received in a revolutionary way, building upon the idea of packets of data. Remarking on the process of designing the protocol, Vint Cerf described the problem of trying to connect multiple networks:

The packet sizes weren't the same. The data rates were different. The addressing structures were different. And yet we wanted to assure that the military would have the ability to deploy computers anywhere it needed them, and communicate uniformly across this multiplicity of different packet switched networks. That became known, at least to Bob and me, as the Internet problem, as we were trying to connect nets to each other.[22]

In 1974, Cerf and Kahn published their paper on the design of the internet. Now it was time to take their protocol for a test drive.

* * *

Keith Uncapher worked with Paul Baran at RAND on packet switching and routing, the original architecture of the internet's node structure. In 1972, Uncapher created the Information Sciences Institute (ISI) with affiliation to the University of Southern California (USC), but it primarily purposed as a West Coast research lab for ARPA and eventually the site of pivotal milestones in the internet's evolution. The institute played a central role in the internet's transition from a military technology to a public one and the development of protocols for email and our domain name system—such as .com, .edu, and .gov. For decades, the country's entire domain name registry was organized on computers at USC-ISI.

---

22 *Vinton Cerf, "Oral-History."*

The institute's most significant contribution centered around a singular moment in 1977 when Cerf and Kahn demonstrated the initial three-network test of TCP, featuring ARPANET, a satellite-based network that connected the United States to Europe, and a radio-powered system that originally helped the Hawaiian Islands stay in communication with each other. A test message began at Stanford over radio, traveled to BBN in Boston via the ARPANET, then to Norway via satellite, over to London, and then back to USC-ISI in California. In total, the 94,000-mile, three-network journey suffered zero data loss, proving it was now possible for any computer to connect with any computer using this unified protocol.[23]

Everybody at USC-ISI was thrilled with the results but had some ideas to improve and finalize the protocol before global adoption. Researchers split TCP message routing into two protocols: TCP would be responsible for breaking messages into little blocks and then reassembling them, putting packets together in the right order, and Internet Protocol (IP) would be responsible for the routing. With the new internet ready for implementation, early adopters jumped right in—Bill Joy started the semiconductor giant Sun Microsystems with all its machines equipped with TCP/IP for internet accessibility, putting the internet in the hands of businesses everywhere by 1983. When learning stories about the internet's origins, we observe a permanence and proliferation of internet protocols once they achieve utility

---

23 *Hafner and Lyon, Wizards.*

and consensus—the worldwide web's protocol is over 30 years old, email's protocol is over 40 years old, and TCP/IP remains the internet's protocol backbone over 50 years later. These early protocols birthed the Information Age—all three are used by billions of people every single day.

CHAPTER 6

A DOLLAR REBORN

H IGH IN THE SWISS ALPS, TRICKLES OF WATER FROM MELTING snow gather momentum to become Europe's most important economic artery, the Rhine River. During the Roman Empire, settlements, trading posts, castles, and great wealth were built along the Rhine, and its importance to European commerce continues today. The first major city along this important European river on its way from the Alps to the North Sea is Basel. In 1225, the first bridge was built over the Rhine in Basel, beginning its tenure as a highly trafficked European trading crossroads.

In short order, Basel also became a banking hub. The town attracted entrepreneurs and great thinkers, leveraged its geographic centrality, and became a place of business for moneychangers. It is also believed that Basel was home to the original Swiss practice of banking secrecy, in which banks kept private all client information despite potential prying eyes of foreign governments. Basel's deep banking history and its role as a gateway to Western Europe made it the ideal host for the Bank for International Settlements (BIS), founded in 1930 and headquartered in a town that was destined to be the international center for monetary coordination. This chapter documents the *fifth and sixth steps* toward credit-system dominance—how gold was removed from currency, leaving a purely credit-money system in its wake, and why banks today self-regulate and are mostly unanswerable to the public.

The United States was a latecomer to the central banking system, establishing the Federal Reserve long after other nation-states—the Fed is centuries younger than the Bank of England and 113 years younger than the Bank of France. After getting the Federal Reserve System in place, American and European bankers pushed for an international organization that bridged central banks together to help address potential imbalances. During World War I, the Bank of England, Bank of France, and Federal Reserve all had direct telegraph lines with each other to enhance communication, driven by crises during the previous century. The central banks hoped for cooperation to avoid seizures in activity that could bring global finance to a standstill, but they didn't have an official alliance or mechanism through which to fashion an emergency response. At a small home-based gathering located in Long Island, New York, in 1927, heads of the Federal Reserve, Bank of England, and German Reichsbank met to figure out how to bring these major institutions closer together.

Montagu Norman, head of the Bank of England, and Benjamin Strong, the Federal Reserve Bank of New York's first leader and one of the masquerading duck hunters from Jekyll Island, led the meeting. Dear friends and staunch allies, the two men were determined to see through a plan for an international financial institution between central banks. The Fed and Bank of England had recently strengthened their relationship after the Fed's support during the UK's currency crises in the aftermath of World War I, but Norman desired a more formal coordination mechanism. Preliminary agreements were made for the inception of a central bank of central banks called the Bank for International Settlements, but the Federal Reserve was prohibited by US law from participating in such an organization. This legal hurdle led to J.P. Morgan and Citibank contributing the starting capital to the BIS on behalf of the American government.

In 1930, an official agreement was signed in Rome that yielded a Switzerland-domiciled BIS, which initially took on the role of administering reparation payments and coordinating communication between central banks, but its role would evolve greatly over time. The charter itself displayed an incredible range of diplomatic immunities and international permissions reserved for only the highest-order intergovernmental organizations. The BIS later assisted both sides of World War II in gold transfers, giving it a historical black eye in its connection with the German Reichsbank.

In 1961, the hidden treasure backing all dollar credits was a stockpile of gold held at the US Bullion Depository at Fort Knox in Kentucky. This precious metal reserve powered millions of interbank messages every day, driven by people's belief that dollar credits were linked to gold. But by the 1960s, this illusion was unraveling as the hidden treasure dwindled.

From 1958 to 1960, the United States lost 22% of its gold holdings to conversions, a process by which an official entity submits dollar credits—sometimes suitcases of paper money—to the US Treasury and requests to redeem physical gold. When the US established deposit insurance, its goal was to prevent customers from running on their banks, but now, the country was experiencing a different type of run. The 22% decline in gold holdings was seen as a *run on the dollar* in the eyes of newly elected President John F. Kennedy and his closest economic advisors.[24]

The American government panicked. Continued conversions would cause US gold reserves to disappear in a matter of years—a run on the government's gold instead of on a bank's currency didn't have deposit insurance to stop it. The official price of gold rested at $35 per ounce, but the London price crept up, exposing the dollar's declining reputation now that American hidden treasure was being depleted. The worrying drop in gold at Fort Knox and the gold price rising toward $40 were signs that the link between the dollar and gold was suffering a dissolution of belief. Alfred Hayes, president of the Federal Reserve Bank of New York, flew to Basel out of necessity. Hayes adamantly refused to leave Switzerland without securing an agreement between central banks to manipulate the price of gold back down to $35 hoping to preserve the mind trick that credits were backed by gold.

Usage of US currency had arguably grown *too much* outside the United States—an unforeseen and poorly understood

---

24 *Younger, "Eurodollars."*

phenomenon by members of the Fed. Hayes' visit to the BIS in 1961 was a notable event because senior officials of the New York Fed did not habitually attend BIS meetings. Known in financial circles as the "Basel Club" during the era of greater financial coordination starting in 1958, leading central bankers from around the world would gather at the BIS every few weeks to discuss interest rates, exchange rates, the state of the economy, and trade relationships. At these meetings, policies weren't mandated down to individual central banks—instead, central bankers gathered in Basel to coordinate policy, with the goal of maintaining credit-system dominance. New York Fed deputy Charles Coombs, who visited Basel before Hayes, called the BIS "an ideal meeting place for central bankers seeking refuge for quiet and confidential discussion."[25]

Many BIS officials and participants during the era were strong supporters of a gold-linked credit system and sought a solution that would allow it to continue. They followed Hayes' leadership into establishing a Gold Pool, a scheme imposed by central bankers to prevent the price of gold from rising beyond $35. Hayes flew back to New York, pleased at the result of the meeting. The Gold Pool endured for seven years but would not last, and neither would gold's fixed price. During the operation of the Gold Pool, French head of state Charles de Gaulle believed the dollar system to be excessively overleveraged and decided his dollar claims would be better protected if converted to gold. In a direct confrontation

---

25 *Toniolo, Cooperation.*

of US geopolitical power, France withdrew over $3 billion of bullion from American reserves during the 1960s, sending a message that the US government's gold stock would not withstand the sheer quantity of dollar credit circulating the globe. Spain joined France in converting credits to gold.[26]

A speculative attack by banks using dollar credits against the British pound in late 1967 sent the price of gold firmly above $40 in London trading, causing authorities to abandon the Gold Pool in 1968. US policymakers recognized that they needed to supply enough dollars to foreign markets to ensure a global economy centered around American currency, but not too many such that owners of dollar credits preferred to switch back to gold. Striking this balance proved insurmountable, however, as famously predicted as early as 1959 by economist Robert Triffin in front of Congress. An increase in the gold dollar-price in London and the conversion of currency held in foreign official accounts into gold started to break the dollar-gold link. The penultimate *fifth step* in establishing credit-system dominance came when President Richard Nixon closed the US Treasury's gold window in 1971—the permanent end to hidden treasure. Now all money—bank deposits and high-powered money such as central bank reserves—could be created from thin air without any worry that a creditor might try to trade credits for precious metal.[27]

---

26 *Time Magazine, "De Gaulle v. The Dollar."*

27 *Philip Cagan, "Stock of Money."*

*   *   *

The dismissal of hidden treasure brought about a new ruler. Without gold as a discipline on the issuance of currency and credits, banks prepared the credit system for universal hegemony. Governments and central banks thought that reserve ratios and capital requirements for banks satisfied a societal demand for prudence within the public utility, but banks obeyed their own rules and continually invented ways to skirt regulations. The size of the global financial industry exploded after 1971. Free-floating currencies resulted in London banks settling trades with fresh Eurodollars, permeating credits in sizes never imagined throughout the world. An oil shock in 1973 sent energy prices, and therefore demand for US currency, soaring, reinforcing the need for less-regulated dollar banking in Europe to satisfy trade financing needs for energy consumers. In an all-out eruption of bank credit, the world underwent a chasmic transition from an equity-based system to a debt-based system, wherein debt assets became more desirable than gold.[28]

Our *sixth step* to lock in credit-system dominance and complete the dollar's reincarnation occurred after the collapse of a German bank called Bankhaus Herstatt in 1974, when the world's most powerful nations gathered at the BIS to announce their unwavering support for the Eurodollar system. Despite the bank's modest size, a protracted seizure of the global financial system occurred after German

---

28 Younger, "Origin Story."

regulators closed it before it could make good on credits owed to American counterparties.[29] The two largest banks in the world, Chase and Citibank, stopped processing wires because they felt completely blindsided by who else might default from the Eurodollar realm. Bank wires globally ground to a complete and disastrous halt.

After a two-day financial standstill, the seizure was slowly unwoven by Citibank, which restarted the flow of money. The Herstatt failure rocked the banking system, which had finally encountered the risks building up from a gold-free system of credit creation and sparse transparency. In 1975, meetings at the BIS yielded the first Basel Concordat, a banking protocol that would protect the global banking dollar under any circumstance. Confidence in today's credit system still relies on the decisions made in Basel during that fateful meeting—in 2025, banks will roll out Basel III, the third iteration of global banking regulations and capital adequacy ratios that began after the collapse of Bankhaus Herstatt and a collective realization that if banks don't monitor each other, nobody will.[30] Banks themselves operate under a system of self-regulation and are still devising it today, but most important to them is a political and financial system that immediately remedies credit contraction. Our greatest evidence of the banking cartel's success at establishing a global credit system is inflation, the collapse of the dollar's purchasing power, and its perpetual dilution—$1

---

29 Younger, "Eurodollars."

30 Gabriel Rauterberg and Joshua Younger, "The Hidden Monetary State."

million bought 40 houses in 1971, but today that sum would barely cover the price of two.

CHAPTER 7

CRYPTO

A S THE UNITED STATES STOOD ON THE CUSP OF DEVELOPING ARPANET—an interconnected network of computers driven by innovations from the private and academic sectors under Defense Department coordination—another, far lesser-known corner of the government had, for the first time ever, lost its cloak of mystery. When President Harry Truman created the National Security Agency (NSA) in 1952, he did so by issuing a classified Defense Department memo. His top-secret order wasn't publicly divulged until a document was published in 1957, a full five years later, that even acknowledged the agency's existence—giving it the nickname "No Such Agency." Once people saw the NSA's facility in Maryland, they also started calling it the "Triple Fence" thanks to its three layers of surrounding electronic fencing.

After NSA defectors fled to the Soviet Union and revealed many of the agency's operational secrets, David Kahn published a detailed book in 1967 documenting the mission of the agency—communications intelligence—and its cryptographic methods. *The Codebreakers* was a groundbreaking exposé of the National Security Agency and the most comprehensive history of cryptography ever written at that time. The NSA tried to stop the book's publishing in several ways but backed down after Kahn agreed to a few specific deletions: "It didn't really hurt the book, so I took the three things out. But I insisted that we put in a statement to the effect that the book had been submitted to the Department of Defense."[31]

The world of modern cryptography got its first public sunlight after *The Codebreakers* hit bookshelves, largely because knowledge of the entire field had rested behind closed doors. Many today associate the word *crypto* with crypto*currency*, but the term originally describes the field of *cryptography*, which is the ancient art or practice of writing in code, found across empires from the altered hieroglyphics of Egypt to encoded military messages of ancient Greece. Crypto knowledge spread rapidly throughout the academic community once computer science students and professors finished reading their copies of Kahn's trailblazing book.

As information became more digital, data needed a way to protect itself from intruders while in transit. Hackers can steal information, but if that information is disguised in a way that makes it unintelligible to read, theft becomes a wasted effort. This is the core concept behind encryption, which is cryptography applied to the protection of digital data by scrambling it—an *encrypted* message looks nonsensical and is functionally useless unless it is *decrypted*. Today, modern encryption protects nuclear codes, bank transactions, and even our text messages.

---

31 *Steven Levy, Crypto.*

Academics studying encryption experienced an intense frustration with the NSA, as nearly 100% of all cryptography research happened behind the Triple Fence. There was no private enterprise of cryptography before Kahn's book, and every single graduate of merit in the field went directly to work for the agency. The government classified all relevant academic research, stifling the private sector's academic pursuit of crypto. *The Codebreakers* had set research scientists on a collision course with the US government.

* * *

When Larry Roberts started working for ARPA, coworkers noticed his obsession with navigating the building's zig-zag hallways. As he traversed the Pentagon, the turns he would take would be known as "Larry's route" because of his uncanny ability to find the quickest path between any two offices in the massive and sprawling building. His brain worked in powerful ways, able to see things others couldn't. In the beginning months of ARPANET's cross-country connections, Roberts envisioned the problem of secure communication posing an immediate challenge to the young network—sending messages and data privately required encryption. He asked the NSA for help, but the agency outright declined, as it likely did not want any of its proprietary encryption technology to fall outside the Triple Fence. To the NSA, crypto was a matter of national security and existed within a military-like domain.

Determined to find a solution, Roberts asked computer scientist and early applied cryptographer George Purdy to create an encryption system utilizing password protection for the ARPANET in 1971, the inaugural example of combining crypto with the internet. Despite Purdy's contribution, digital communication still severely lacked secure cryptosystems. Roberts contacted his friend John McCarthy, who is most famous for introducing the term *artificial intelligence* to the computer science community in 1956. McCarthy was a pioneer in mathematics and computing, achieving his doctorate from Princeton in 1951, and his theories were instrumental in the early days of ARPA's network construction. He contributed research from his Stanford AI Lab (SAIL), which he founded in 1973. At SAIL, McCarthy hired the man who would take on the fight for the private use of crypto—Whitfield Diffie.

Diffie dropped out of MIT while studying computer science, eventually finding his way to California and McCarthy's AI Lab. Like many of his peers, Diffie loved *The Codebreakers*, but his obsession and fascination with Kahn's masterpiece elevated his passion for crypto from others. A friend of Diffie's recalled, "If you invited him to dinner, he'd come with *The Codebreakers*." Diffie maintained that he "read it more carefully than anyone had ever read it, like the Vedas." He described his quest to spread the crypto good word:

I was living out of my car, driving around the country talking to anyone who knew anything about cryptography. I had this old Datsun 510, and I just went from place to place, sleeping in the back seat, reading everything I could find. The NSA had a monopoly on cryptographic knowledge, and I was determined to break it. Every now and then I'd find someone who knew something interesting, and I'd stay for a while, learning what I could.[32]

Diffie met Stanford professor Marty Hellman in 1974 when Hellman joined Stanford as a part-time researcher. The two quickly bonded over a shared interest in cryptography and were eager to explore solutions that might exist only within the NSA, or perhaps nowhere at all. Hellman described his relief after meeting Diffie and discovering he was not alone in his passion for finding cryptographic solutions:

It was a meeting of the minds. I'd been working in a vacuum and was feeling, 'Is this really worth it?' I was really getting concerned about whether this was going to lead anywhere.

After two tireless years of research and tinkering, Whitfield Diffie and Marty Hellman published their paper "Multiuser Cryptographic Techniques" to propose ideas around digital authentication and secure communication. The paper didn't contain the cryptographic solutions themselves, but it inspired like minds to iterate on the concepts, build software, and get in touch. Almost immediately, Hellman received a letter from UC Berkeley researcher Ralph Merkle:

---

32 *Levy, Crypto.*

About three days ago, a copy of your working paper, 'Multiuser Cryptographic Techniques' fell into my hands... I'm glad to know there's someone else who's interested in the problem.[33]

Merkle's innovative brainpower helped Diffie and Hellman discover powerful crypto solutions that could be applied to everyday communication. The team's 1976 paper "New Directions in Cryptography" claimed to put the private sector "on the brink of a revolution in cryptography" and fired shots directly at the NSA with its conclusion:

We hope this will inspire others to work in this fascinating area in which participation has been discouraged in the recent past by a nearly total government monopoly.[34]

Ralph Merkle became immortalized in crypto history after publishing "Protocols for Public Key Cryptosystems"— cited in the bitcoin whitepaper, published by its author Satoshi Nakamoto 28 years later. With its power to inspire young and ambitious cryptographers, Merkle's paper set off a crypto war with the US government.

---

33 *Levy, Crypto.*

34 *Whitfield Diffie and Martin Hellman, "New Directions in Cryptography."*

In 1977, Ron Rivest of MIT, Adi Shamir of the Weizmann Institute in Israel, and Leonard Adelman of USC published an encryption algorithm called RSA, using the first letter of each of their last names as the algorithm's name. RSA was the first implementation of the New Directions paper and was directly inspired by the trio of Diffie, Hellman, and Merkle; it showed the world the power of data encryption available to the masses. The implications of this new tool were stunning, and the feeling that power had sifted through the fingers of the NSA into the hands of the public was palpable.

David Chaum was one of the earliest adopters of these new cryptographic tools. He participated in the first ever crypto conference at the University of California—Santa Barbara in 1981 and took personal responsibility over ensuring the gatherings continued. Diffie, Hellman, Merkle, Rivest, Shamir, Adelman, and many of the world's top cryptographers gathered under the same roof for the first time, delivered papers, and hung out together on the beach.[35] A crypto community was finally coming together and building personal relationships.

Participants in Crypto 1981 left feeling energized. They felt they had entered a winnable fight against the NSA, inspiring Chaum to mail out letters to get people to return for Crypto 1982 after the conference's first-year success. He learned that the government was trying to prevent crypto

---

35 Aaron van Wirdum, *The Genesis Book.*

conferences from taking place and proceeded to use hand-written letters to hide any evidence of electronic or telephone communication between cryptographers. Chaum feared their efforts would potentially be prosecuted as illegal—fears that later played out in the 1990s.

Santa Barbara's shoreline played host to some of the earliest conversations that can be tied to bitcoin's creation. The two conferences gave the spotlight to cryptography, allowing researchers to emerge from obscurity within mathematics departments and take charge of their own science. Most importantly for our story, Chaum's obsession with digital cash and private transactions inspired minds that directly or indirectly built bitcoin's components long before it existed. The 28-year period between the Crypto 1981 and Satoshi Nakamoto's whitepaper unfolded every scientific and cultural breakthrough required for bitcoin's construction—except the ingenuity of its creator.

CHAPTER 8

BITCOIN'S PRELUDE

"The computer can be used as a tool to liberate and protect people, rather than to control them."[36]

-HAL FINNEY, 1992

A CRYPTO WAR COMMENCED IN THE 1980S, PITTING THE OPEN computer science community against intelligence agencies within the US government, which had classified cryptography as a weapons-grade munition in a bid to maintain its control over the field. But tireless internet idealists guaranteed our networked future by pursuing innovation and passionately fighting the US government to secure their right to use encryption across jurisdictions.

Cryptographers at the time knew they were engaged in a David-versus-Goliath battle, but the rejection of government control over technology united these pioneers and enthusiasts from the first days of the internet. This cohort believed that centralization of information, control of communication channels, and surveillance of communication were all a threat to free society, and finally addressable with cryptography.

---

36 *Hal Finney, "Why remailers..."*

Each individual victory against the government in the crypto war helped protect private encryption and made it possible for information to flow freely across telephone lines, borders, and oceans via the internet. These victories also paved the way for the greatest innovation of our time— one that allowed money, like information, to move without the constraints of governments and banks as its sentry. The invention of bitcoin hands power back to the people and weakens the stronghold banks have kept over society's entire experience with money. Just as sending messages no longer depends on government-controlled postal services, value transfer no longer relies on bank routing. Bitcoin is the great equalizer.

Its assembly, like any well-oiled machine, requires several moving parts. In this chapter, we identify the first six of *seven key ingredients* that laid the foundation for bitcoin's system of peer-to-peer electronic cash.

Bitcoin Ingredient #1: Hash functions

Ralph Merkle's revolutionary cryptography work contained something critical to bitcoin's build—the *hash function*. Hash functions scramble and convert electronic data into a fixed size; they underpin modern encryption. One of the original non-NSA academic cryptographers, Ron Rivest—the "R" in RSA—developed MD2 in 1989, the first widely adopted application of Merkle's theories and the debut of a private sector encryption product. With MD2, people could at last encrypt data into something uncrackable. Rivest's work showed the field that crypto can provide both security and proof that something had occurred. The power of a hashing function is such that once performed, it is practically impossible to reverse-engineer the output to find the original input. In 1993, the NSA released its own standard for cryptographic hash functions called Secure Hash Algorithm, the predecessor for its subsequent standard SHA-2, which is used today in banking, military operations, and bitcoin.

The most powerful feature of these modern hashing functions is the improbability of reverse-engineering them. Finding the original data after it has gone through a powerful cryptographic hash function such as SHA-2 is less likely than finding the correct grain of sand among a thousand Earths. Thus, it is not impossible, but improbable, because one could theoretically guess the original data that created such a result. Given the hash, however, what lies on the other side is basically unattainable—this fundamental obscurity of information forms the foundation of modern cryptography.[37]

Bitcoin Ingredient #2: Time-stamps

Satoshi Nakamoto cited eight papers in the original bitcoin proposal. Chronologically, the first was a 1957 work from William Feller on probability theory, which holds together bitcoin's ingenious design. Next was Ralph Merkle's foundational 1980 paper on public key cryptosystems. Three of the final six featured W. Scott Stornetta and Stuart Haber.

---

37   *Hallam Stevens, "Birth of the Hashing Algorithm."*

In 1991, Stornetta and Haber published "How To Time-Stamp a Digital Document" in the *Journal of Cryptology*—they had figured out how to connect hashes together in a sequence to prove the order in which events occurred. Bitcoin's blockchain—blocks of transactions linked together through hashes—mirrors the design pioneered by Stornetta and Haber, which was created to prove the chronological order of published documents. In their abstract, the pair described why the time-stamping data is important for transparency in electronic communication:

> *The prospect of a world in which all text, audio, picture, and video documents are in digital form on easily modifiable media raises the issue of how to certify when a document was created or last changed. The problem is to time-stamp the data, not the medium. We propose computationally practical procedures for digital time-stamping of such documents so that it is infeasible for a user either to back-date or to forward-date his document, even with the collusion of a time-stamping service.[38]*

Their idea was updated in 1993 and again in 1997, and all three papers were cited by Satoshi Nakamoto. The authors presented their idea as an attempt to address problems with data security, not money, and admitted they did not envision time-stamping would contribute to a solution to decentralized electronic cash.[39]

---

38 *Haber and Stornetta, "Time-stamp," Journal of Cryptology.*

39 *van Wirdum, Genesis Book.*

Bitcoin Ingredient #3: Cypherpunks

Bitcoin is an ideology. It's a new idea: that money must not be linked to government, banks, credit, or a physical commodity—but to an internet protocol. The idea sounds radical, but that is because it doesn't have any precedent. Early bitcoin adopters signaled that their time and computing power were worth storing in a new form of money—a declaration rooted in the steadfast belief that an alternative to credit-system dominance must exist. Mistrust in power underlies millennia of political conflict, and it would be unfair to categorize bitcoin's story as anything different. A deep desire to separate money from governments and banks elicited bitcoin, which should be viewed as a *political effort* in its creation just as much as a technological one. Its elegant technical solution tends to disguise the underlying political agenda of its creator.

* * *

In the early days of the crypto war, an egregiously overreaching US Senate bill was proposed in 1991 targeting encryption and mandating that the government be granted abilities to decrypt all private communication in the name of national security. With tensions already building over repeated run-ins with the NSA, the bill infuriated cryptographers. When Phil Zimmermann read the proposed legislation, the urge to fight back overwhelmed him. A practitioner of RSA's pioneering encryption, Zimmermann built a privacy tool that leveraged RSA and MD5, an encryption algorithm that had evolved from MD2. Upon completion, Zimmermann published Pretty Good Privacy (PGP), the public's first military-grade privacy tool:

> *It was this bill that led me to publish PGP electronically for free that year, shortly before the measure was defeated after vigorous protest by civil libertarians and industry groups.*[40]

Before any outside developer reached out to Zimmermann, Hal Finney offered to help.

Harold Thomas Finney II loved computers and long-distance running under the bright California sun. Born in a small agricultural town in Central California, Finney took residence in Santa Barbara after finishing his engineering degree at Caltech. He began his career developing video games for Mattel but eventually found and fell in love with cryptography. Hal Finney described himself as obsessive—he would program for days at a stretch when toying with software that fascinated him. He helped Zimmermann improve the PGP code and wrote documentation that made the privacy tool more usable by the masses. Zimmermann and Finney embodied the cypherpunk, a term requiring some California history to explain its meaning.

---

40 *Philip Zimmermann, "Why I Wrote PGP."*

*   *   *

Max O'Conner graduated from the University of Oxford before gaining acceptance to the PhD program in philosophy at USC and moving to Los Angeles in 1987. The transition from Great Britain to California suited him—the forward-thinking culture fit his approach to life. It was in California where he decided to take on a new last name that would capture his desire to never stop learning: "More."

Befriending a futurist at USC initiated Max More into the California custom of thinking outside the box. He started a journal named *Extropy* in 1988, capturing the readership of brilliant scientists and engineers, including cryptographer Ralph Merkle and Nobel Prize winner in physics Richard Feynman.[41] The magazine connected people who genuinely believed the future would bring a better world—a more advanced society that would benefit from scientific innovation. As this *Extropian* community grew, one topic always found its way back into the discussion: digital cash. This culminated in a 1995 issue of *Extropy* fully dedicated to exploring the topic, wherein More proclaimed that digital cash could upend the way the world works.

Two of the issue's readers were Tim May and Eric Hughes. May had snagged one of the early ARPANET accounts at UC Santa Barbara in 1973, envisioning the internet's potential before it truly gained traction. After landing a job at Intel at 22 years old, he quickly achieved semiconductor superstardom

41   *van Wirdum, Genesis Book.*

by discovering a flaw in Intel's packaging, turning his stock options in the company into a handsome retirement package by age 34. While enjoying the fruits of his ingenuity, May preferred spending time reading books on politics and economics, dreaming up a future in which technology allowed people to maintain privacy from governments. His friend Eric Hughes had just returned to the US from Amsterdam after joining— and quickly resigning from—Crypto conference host David Chaum's privacy-forward digital currency company DigiCash. Cryptography was utilized in DigiCash transactions, but the transactions themselves were still tied to a Dutch company using traditional deposit banking in Europe.

The company attracted some of the most enthusiastic minds in digital currency, but Hughes left because DigiCash didn't fit his ideology; it relied on gatekeepers instead of trying to break down walls. May and Hughes began organizing meetings to pursue cryptography and privacy efforts in ways aligned with their vision of the future, welcoming those who wanted to empower the individual. Before long, the group had a name: cypherpunks—a combination of the cryptology-inspired word 'cipher' and the word 'cyberpunk,' a term to describe a genre of novels dealing in dystopian science-fictional worlds. "A Cypherpunk's Manifesto" by Hughes laid out the following proclamation:

We must come together and create systems which allow anonymous transactions to take place. People have been defending their own privacy for centuries with whispers, darkness, envelopes, closed doors, secret handshakes, and couriers. *The technologies of the past did not allow for strong privacy, but electronic technologies do.*[42]

Bitcoin Ingredient #4: United States Constitution

Phil Zimmermann believed it was the people's right under the First Amendment to pursue mathematically based tools for private communication, despite the US government's best efforts. When the US government launched a criminal investigation into Phil Zimmermann, it charged him with exporting munitions for publishing PGP as a book, classifying PGP's encryption as a weapon. Protests took unconventional forms—a young cryptographer by the name of Adam Back printed shirts with a few lines of the RSA encryption algorithm and encouraged those wearing it to cross borders and demonstrate the preposterous nature of preventing the export of computer code. As a result of the public outcry, the government eventually dropped charges in 1996.

In levying a case against Zimmermann, the government inspired cryptographers to go on the offensive in the crypto war. Daniel Bernstein studied math at New York University and, like many other aspiring cryptographers before him, came to California to advance his studies. While at UC Berkeley, he developed a strong encryption system that he felt required the attention of authorities. Bernstein responsibly approached the US State Department to ask for policies

---

42   *Eric Hughes, "A Cypherpunk's Manifesto."*

and procedures around publishing the code, but instead of receiving guidance on the proper licensing, he was instructed to register as an arms dealer and told that foreign classmates in his graduate program would be required to attain government approval to interact with the code in an academic setting. Blindsided by the restrictive encryption-as-a-weapon stance, Bernstein took to battle. He viewed software code as a form of speech and believed that government restrictions on electronic communication infringed on his Constitutional rights. Bernstein sued the State Department for violating his First Amendment rights, and three consecutive federal judges ruled in his favor. The US judicial system argued and upheld that computer code and mathematical models fall within the category of speech and are protected under the First Amendment, a precedent that ended the government's monopoly over encryption.

Bitcoin Ingredient #5: Proof-of-work

During the height of the crypto war, Adam Back's political statement protest shirt equated software code with free speech. As an extension of how he poetically defended cypherpunk ideals, Back was also obsessed with decentralizing currency. His direct contribution to bitcoin was a cryptographic incentive structure called Hashcash—the eighth and chronologically final citation in the bitcoin whitepaper.

Here is a simplified explanation of how Hashcash works. Imagine you want to send an email to your friend, but his inbox is behind a locked door. To send the message, you need a bit of luck. Imagine a stack of cards numbered 1 to 5,000. If you pick a card with a number 5 or lower, you win, and the email is sent. Otherwise, you lose, and the email does not go through. In this game, there are only five winning cards and 4,995 losing ones.

In Hashcash, email senders must perform hashes (picking cards) until the output falls within a specified range (pick a card with a very small number on it). A winning hash will have several *leading zeroes*. Using our example of 5,000 cards, a winning card might look like this: 0004. Notice how the card has three leading zeros? In cryptographic hashing, a winning hash has many more leading zeros—something like this: 0000000000000042859. Generating a winning hash on a computer, just like picking cards over and over again to find one with a small number, takes time and energy—it requires *work*. Back suggested that if people used email addresses that required *proof* that work has been completed before messages are let through, spam would become costly and therefore unlikely. A spammer can send countless emails at a very low cost, but if the spammer's computer had to perform millions of hash functions just to send each email, the time, electricity, and computing power required would probably act as a deterrent.

Hashcash demonstrated the concept of proof-of-work but didn't result in a digital currency. Back understood that because crypto tools were utilized for transactions between users, reliance on banks for final settlement left companies such as DigiCash exposed to bureaucratic risk, banking relationships, and legal action. He never worked for David Chaum's DigiCash, but did discuss online how only a *disconnected system* could lead to an effective electronic cash, which must be both distributed and scarce. The solution was more elusive than anybody might have imagined.

Bitcoin Ingredient #6: Distributed Time-stamping

Inspired by the early vision of David Chaum, Nick Szabo pursued a career at DigiCash in Amsterdam. Like Eric Hughes, however, he didn't feel the project was cypherpunk enough and came back to California. An early participant in the Hughes and Tim May group meetings in California's Bay Area, Szabo wrote prolifically on digital property rights and encryption-based security. Szabo designed *bit gold* as a system that coordinated between nodes, using distributed time-stamping and proof-of-work to keep track of title transfer. His concept, a very similarly structured group of cryptographic incentives to bitcoin, was never released as software for people to try. Thankfully, there was somebody else ready to go the distance.

CHAPTER 9

MAGIC INGREDIENT #7

"I've developed a new open source P2P e-cash system called
Bitcoin. It's completely decentralized, with no central server
or trusted parties, because everything is based on crypto
proof instead of trust."[43]
-Satoshi Nakamoto, February 11, 2009

Satoshi Nakamoto appeared on the cryptography scene as if from nowhere. Nobody had met, collaborated, or communicated with this new entity, but he donned all the hallmarks of a cypherpunk—somebody who used cryptography to empower the individual. The seventh and final ingredient in bitcoin's recipe is its designer and software developer, Satoshi Nakamoto.

Benjamin Franklin, Alexander Hamilton, James Madison, John Jay, and Thomas Jefferson helped found the United States of America—these Founding Fathers often used pseudonyms in their writing. Hiding behind an alias allowed these revolutionaries to speak freely without worrying about the King of England targeting them for stoking political dissent. These young, whip-smart Americans understood that

---

43 *Satoshi Nakamoto, "Bitcoin: Open Source," 11 Feb 2009.*

spotlighting their compelling ideas was more important than standing in the spotlight for personal glory.

To promote their ideas, Hamilton, Madison, and Jay adopted the alias *Publius* and put forth the *Federalist Papers*, which brought attention to the need for a United States Constitution. The group underscored the very notion that ideas can and should dominate the discussion, so that who writes them doesn't detract observers from the underlying proposals.

Satoshi Nakamoto's story can be compared to the Founding Fathers—the pursuit of freedom from centralized, external control motivated anonymous individuals to circumvent it. Hamilton and his contemporaries chose this route because they were fighting the English crown, while Satoshi attempted to circumvent financial institutions, targeting banks instead of a far-away monarchy. His whitepaper, titled "Bitcoin: A Peer-to-Peer Electronic Cash System," did not express a desire to end banks, credit, and governments but provided an alternative to the existing *centralized* currency system by utilizing the internet and cryptography.

Satoshi knew he had created something unique, using proof-of-work in an imaginative way. The first person who Satoshi contacted—that we know of—was Adam Back. Back authored Hashcash, the only citation from the bitcoin whitepaper explicitly discussed in its text. In the spirit of the Founding Fathers, Satoshi chose anonymity when contacting Back, writing the bitcoin paper, and releasing its code because of reasons only known to Satoshi. Instead, we use his written correspondences during the three years of his public interactions to speculate. In 2008, there was no way to know that bitcoin would be worth over $2 trillion as a network by 2025, making greed an unlikely reason to launch bitcoin anonymously. More likely, Satoshi knew that in order for people to examine the merit of a decentralized digital currency, it would help if the center of the debate was the idea instead of the creator. Sixteen years into bitcoin's existence, the Satoshi Nakamoto alias has made no attempt to reveal its identity.

* * *

Email allows two people on separate continents to exchange messages instantly, allowing back-and-forth communication that a century ago required months and ocean-bound ships. Over the internet, messages do not travel through a central authority, but via distributed protocols—email is *decentralized* mail. Bitcoin decentralizes money transfer because, unlike David Chaum's DigiCash, it uses its own currency—a complete break from banks, wires, and credits. By relying on banks to keep track of our money, we give them the power to create—and thereby dilute—the very money which we entrust to them. The problem bitcoin's technology addresses, quite succinctly, is that banking lacks an issuance protocol.

"I believe I've worked through all those little details over the last year and a half while coding it, and there were a lot of them," wrote Satoshi to the cryptography mailing list shortly after he published his paper on October 31, 2008, revealing when he might have started his bitcoin project.[44] Before we delve into the paper's text, what prompted him to begin in the first place?

Using his communications after publishing the whitepaper for inference, we hypothesize that the inception of bitcoin was triggered by perpetual monetary dilution and the omnipotence of banking power, and its timing spurred on by the beginning of a three-year global financial crisis. In the days before megabank JPMorgan Chase acquired 84-year-old Wall Street darling Bear Stearns, we learned how the flailing investment bank's credit extension defied historical precedents for leverage. In a traditional fractional, credit-money system, an imbalance between reserves and deposits occurs when money is lent into existence. A bank with $1 million in capital habitually issues $10 million in loans, leading to $10 million in deposits that are only backed by $1 million in equity—this is the money multiplier effect explained in Chapter 4. Another way to state this is that banks are leveraged in a way that a 9% decline in assets coming from defaults by its customers can wipe out the bank. Bear Stearns expanded credit through non-deposit instruments such as securitization and derivatives, bringing its leverage ratio over 30 to 1, meaning that a mere 3% decline in assets could potentially cause the bank to fail.

Embarrassingly lax mortgage standards during the mid-2000s resulted in global banks holding massive portfolios

---

44 *Satoshi Nakamoto, "Bitcoin P2P e-Cash Paper," #014863.*

of securities that were destined to default. As missed pay-ments from home borrowers turned to underperformance of mortgage-backed securities, the system of Basel-connected, self-regulating banks both within and outside of the United States, was exposed for how much credit had been extended around the world. The emperor—a financial system flush with $1,000 trillion in credit and currency derivatives by 2008, roughly 20 times the size of the entire global economy —or at the time—had no clothes.

* * *

Satoshi Nakamoto emailed Adam Back a little over two months before he published his bitcoin whitepaper.[45]

> *From: satoshi@anonymousspeech.com*
>
> *To: adam@cypherspace.org*
>
> *August 20, 2008*
>
> *Subject: Citation of your Hashcash paper*
>
> *I'm getting ready to release a paper that references your Hashcash paper and I wanted to make sure I have the citation right. Here's what I have:*
>
> *[5] A. Back, "Hashcash - a denial of service counter-measure," http://www.hashcash.org/papers/hashcash.pdf, 2002.*
>
> *I think you would find it interesting, since it finds a new use for hash-based proof-of-work as a way to make e-cash*

---

45   Pete Rizzo, "Adam Back's Complete Emails," Bitcoin Magazine.

work. You can download a pre-release draft at http://
www.upload.ae/file/6157/ecash-pdf.html

Feel free to forward it to anyone else you think would be
interested. I'm also nearly finished with a C++ implemen-
tation to release as open source.

The email concluded with a brief abstract of his paper. Back replied the next day without reading it:

From: Adam Back
To: Satoshi
August 21, 2008
Subject: Re: Citation of your Hashcash paper
Yes citation looks fine, I'll take a look at your paper. You
[may be] aware of the B-money proposal, I guess Google
can find it for you, by Wei Dai which sounds to be some-
what related to your paper. (The b-money idea is just
described concisely on his web page, he didn't write up a
paper).

Adam

An internet search for Wei Dai would reveal that he was a cypherpunk to his core, although very little information about him is publicly available. Dai built a successful career as a security cryptographer at Microsoft, but his heart was else-where—he was just as obsessed with electronic cash and the denationalization of currency as his sovereign-minded peers Hal Finney, Adam Back, and Nick Szabo were. Contributing to cypherpunk mailing lists during the 1990s, Dai published an idea called b-money on his website that described an electronic cash system using Ingredient #5 (proof-of-work) to create new units of money. The online post lacked specifics, however, and was never followed up with software code for users to try. Satoshi replied:

> *Thanks, I wasn't aware of the b-money page, but my ideas start from exactly that point. I'll e-mail him to confirm the year of publication so I can credit him.*
>
> *The main thing my system adds is to also use proof-of-work to support a distributed timestamp server. While users are generating proof-of-work to make new coins for themselves, the same proof-of-work is also supporting the network timestamping.*

This response exuded confidence—Satoshi believed he had concocted a groundbreaking recipe, combining Ingredient #5 (proof-of-work) *and* Ingredient #6 (distributed time-stamping) in a way nobody had tried. Every cypherpunk that lived through the crypto war or was born in its echoes sought the Holy Grail of decentralized electronic cash but not a single one of them had figured it out. Satoshi had, and his conviction was unequivocal. With his citations complete, it was time to share bitcoin with the world.

* * *

"I've been working on a new electronic cash system that's fully peer-to-peer, with no trusted third party," wrote Satoshi Nakamoto when he introduced his paper to the cryptography mailing list. *Fully* peer-to-peer was the emphasis—he had figured out a way to avoid banks *entirely*. The paper began:

> *A purely peer-to-peer version of electronic cash would allow online payments to be sent directly from one party to another without going through a financial institution.*[46]

Until bitcoin, online transactions required financial institutions because the internet didn't have its own currency that could be used without a bank or payments company to keep track of balances and prevent a person from spending the same money twice. Cryptographers named this challenge the *double-spend problem*. To solve the challenge, they would have to solve a computer science conundrum that researchers had been trying to solve for decades—how to coordinate truth online without a trusted third party.

As an example, we envision a Byzantine army preparing to sack a city in the 9th century. It is divided into five factions, each headed by a general. The generals will only be successful in their attack if they strike at precisely the same moment. If only four generals attack and one doesn't, the four attacking factions will be outflanked, outnumbered, and defeated.

---

46 Nakamoto, *"Bitcoin: A Peer-to-Peer Electronic Cash System."*

The generals don't have a secure form of communication, coordinating only by horseback messenger. They are wary of foul play and espionage when communicating by horseback, however, as any single messenger could be a spy. How can they coordinate an attack without risking their lives? Is it possible to pick an exact moment to launch the conquest using messages?

Without a source of truth, it *isn't* possible. This scenario is called the Byzantine Generals Problem, articulated in a computer science paper from Stanford in 1982. For years, cypherpunks tried different ways to create electronic cash but couldn't solve the Byzantine Generals Problem until Satoshi Nakamoto discovered how to *network the truth*. His paper continued:

> *We propose a solution to the double-spending problem using a peer-to-peer network. The network timestamps transactions by hashing them into an ongoing chain of hash-based proof-of-work, forming a record that cannot be changed without redoing the proof-of-work.*[47]

Cryptographic and electronic cash concepts such as Ingredient #5 (proof-of-work) and Ingredient #6 (distributed time-stamping) already existed, but Satoshi combined them with the correct incentives and rules into a system that keeps everybody playing the game. Satoshi had harnessed *game theory*, the study of strategic decisions and their

---

47   *Nakamoto, "Bitcoin: A Peer-to-Peer Electronic Cash System."*

consequences, to bring his software its first users. Players felt they were entering a fair game with clear rules and a level playing field; once they joined, they stayed.

The paper fascinated some of the cryptography mailing list's longest-tenured enthusiasts, especially the PGP-coding and cypherpunk legend Hal Finney. In trying to understand Satoshi's design, which still lacked an explicit ruleset because the code hadn't yet been released, Finney and others voiced their initial concerns—they had a right to be skeptical that some unknown software developer should have discovered an elusive cryptosystem. But Satoshi was equipped with an answer for every critique, indicating how thoroughly he had played out the game theory within bitcoin's structure. "The functional details are not covered in the paper, but the sourcecode is coming soon," Satoshi promised.[48]

Students of our monetary future *must* understand those functional details to properly articulate bitcoin's place in the world, which we argue is the financial asset *least prone to manipulation* humanity has ever seen. Next, we explain how bitcoin works.

---

48 *Nakamoto, "Bitcoin P2P," #014863.*

CHAPTER 10

21,000,000

"I also do think that there is potential value in a form of unforgeable token whose production rate is predictable and can't be influenced by corrupt parties. This would be more analogous to gold than to fiat currencies."[49]

-HAL FINNEY, November 8, 2008

O N JANUARY 8, 2009, TWO MONTHS AFTER THE RELEASE OF his whitepaper, Satoshi Nakamoto shared the earliest working version of the bitcoin software protocol and outlined some of the software's technical components for members of the cryptography mailing list. He didn't immediately expect every prospective user to understand the system he had designed, but Satoshi believed he had discovered *the* solution to the problem of coordinating truth online.

Why is the term cash so pivotal in the context of bitcoin? Cash is a unique type of money in that it doesn't require settlement. A perfect example is a shopkeeper who accepts credit cards and cash. The credit card companies don't pay the shopkeeper for 30 days after a customer spends money. Cash, on the other hand, can easily be spent on expenses

---

49   *Hal Finney, "Bitcoin P2P e-Cash Paper."*

elsewhere moments after it is accepted; once the shopkeeper accepts paper money, it is immediately spendable. Online retailers traditionally couldn't accept cash because no electronic version of it existed, so they outsourced payment processing to companies such as PayPal. PayPal balances aren't cash, but a type of online deposit, or credit. Satoshi invented internet cash with a *peer-to-peer* system, meaning there is no PayPal to track balances and prevent double-spends—everybody connects with one another to prevent a *central authority*.

The software release announcement filled in several of the key details missing from Satoshi's whitepaper—now, he needed to convince people to not only download the software but start producing and using its coins. Without exaggeration, Satoshi needed to create something magical to draw in the world. And he did. This chapter breaks down the seven governing rules of bitcoin's network that attracted its first users.

Bitcoin Protocol Rule #1: Public key cryptography

"Announcing the first release of Bitcoin, a new electronic cash system that uses a peer-to-peer network to prevent double-spending. It's completely decentralized with no server or central authority," Satoshi claimed.[50] Then, he started to explain the system he had designed. "You can get coins by getting someone to send you some," Satoshi wrote, describing a

---

50 *Satoshi Nakamoto, "Bitcoin v0.1 Released," 8 Jan 2009.*

network built for transacting. Coins, what we call 'bitcoin,' or sometimes its financial ticker 'BTC,' circulate via these transactions between users of the network. How they appear in the first place will be discussed in Rule #3.

First, to send somebody coins, one must *own* those coins. So how does ownership work with electronic cash?

Sending bitcoin from Los Angeles to Tokyo utilizes the discovery of public key systems by Whitfield Diffie, Marty Helman, and Ralph Merkle from the late 1970s. Each bitcoin owner has a private key, which is a very long number. The private key's hash is associated with a balance of coins, visible to every bitcoin node. Only the private key's holder can generate a digital signature to authorize the movement of those coins—the act of owning bitcoin is, more specifically, *possession* of a private key that can spend a bitcoin balance. In our example, the person in Tokyo generates a private key only she knows and hashes it twice—once to create a public key for an added layer of security, and a second time to create an address that can be shared with others for receiving transactions, like sharing an email address with somebody. This address cannot be reverse-engineered to find the original private key, because one-way hash algorithms such as the ones used in bitcoin are currently strong enough to secure the codes to nuclear weapons—the strength comes from the irreversibility of these cryptographic hash functions, as explained in Ingredient #1 (public key cryptography). Satoshi chose the most secure algorithms for bitcoin that were available, but also legal to use, thanks to the judicial system victories of Daniel Bernstein and Phil Zimmermann during the 1990s crypto war.

In Tokyo, the recipient shares her address with the sender in Los Angeles. The address is connected to a private key in her possession. The person in Los Angeles sends coins to her in Tokyo by digitally signing a transaction, a process that is comparable to a property-title transfer. Once the transaction is completed, only she can spend the coins because she is the only person with the associated private key, similar to how email messages can only be read by those with the password to the account.

Today, the process of receiving, holding, and spending private keys is managed by digital wallets, whether on a smartphone or a dedicated electronic device. Thanks to early improvements to the bitcoin protocol, multiple private keys can be cryptographically linked together within a single *private seed* that can be converted into 12-word phrases to make them more user-friendly than something that looks like this:

d11b0ce7186db35b02e130fff5ee4db119b2575b6237c-e7150c1dcbf96d8683e9455ecce296883473b5de6b-735d5b4d7f448ee6e037dff65e76cf06382e6eed6

The above private seed, when converted to its 12-word *seed phrase*, appears like this:

idea merit giraffe scissors message exact job praise glance romance thank foil

Private seeds, and their corresponding seed phrases, can be stored on a dedicated device, on a secure smartphone, or even with pen and paper, enabling unparalleled self-reliance for those who desire it. Bitcoin's technology is unbelievably unique—people who can remember twelve consecutive words can store an entire jurisdiction-agnostic fortune in their brain with only some basic memorization.

Bitcoin Protocol Rule #2: Running a node backed by crypto

After explaining that coins circulate by transactions, Satoshi describes where coins come from by guiding new users to "turn on Options -> Generate Coins to run a node and generate blocks."

A node is a computer running the bitcoin software, continuing the terminology used in the internet's foundational protocols TCP/IP and its ARPANET predecessor. When a participant runs the bitcoin software, it joins a network and connects to other bitcoin nodes for information sharing. Transaction data continually updates across the network, so that each node exists on an equally informed footing. If transactions can be sent peer-to-peer "without going through a financial institution" as Satoshi envisioned in his whitepaper, bitcoin enables anyone running a node to join a financial network where they can verify their own money. The software is a system of continuous truth, and each node keeps that truth by downloading every valid bitcoin block.

Bitcoin Protocol Rule #3: Generating blocks

Bitcoin's transaction ledger is a chain of blocks—the blocks are datasets of transactions, and the chain comes from cryptographically linking each block to the next. Each block contains information about changes in ownership of coins: we can think of each block as updating a property deed registry after a county processes new real estate transactions. Generating new blocks is the responsibility of bitcoin *miners*, who process bitcoin transactions and earn new coins by winning cryptographic competitions every few minutes. Creators of new blocks are called bitcoin miners because of the way Satoshi described the process as computationally akin to expending resources to mine gold out of the ground.

Miners assemble a block by first pre-awarding themselves new coins in a *coinbase transaction* from which Coinbase, the first publicly traded bitcoin exchange in the United States, borrowed its name. We'll discuss how much bitcoin is earned in rule #7 as we round out the network's anchoring incentives, or bitcoin's game theory. The coins in each coinbase transaction are the miner's incentive and only become real if the miner gets lucky and generates a block. The miner takes unconfirmed transactions broadcast across the network along with information from the most recent block to prove it's in sync with other nodes, and then enters a race with other miners to extend the chain of blocks, or *blockchain.*

Bitcoin Protocol Rule #4: Proof-of-work difficulty

How does a miner win this race, generate blocks, and earn the new coins? In involves the search for leading zeros we learned about from Hashcash in Ingredient #5 (proof-of-work):

*I made the **proof-of-work difficulty** ridiculously easy to start with, so for a little while in the beginning a typical PC will be able to generate coins in just a few hours.*

Generating a valid block is a game of chance, and the only way to win is to keep trying. In bitcoin mining, the goal of the game is to hash until an extremely low output is found—an output with several leading zeros. Here is a glimpse of the winning block hash with leading zeros that generated block 886,688 in March 2025:

0000000000000000001822dc3db70b75d281687f-8baa10d1818d0703f49feco

Bitcoin mining works similarly to Adam Back's original email spam prevention idea. Remember our stack of cards numbered 1 to 5,000—if you pick a card with a number 5 or less, you win, otherwise, you try again. Bitcoin miners use the cryptographic hash function SHA-256, which was published by the NSA in 2001, as they try over and over to generate a valid block and capture new coins. For bitcoin's next rule, Satoshi introduced an innovative wrinkle to the mechanism of mining—the *difficulty adjustment*.

Bitcoin Protocol Rule #5: Difficulty adjustment

Difficulty is a numerical target that serves as bitcoin's enforcement mechanism. The target tells us how many leading zeros a block hash must have for a miner to generate a block—using our card analogy, a target of 0005 means that only a card saying 0001, 0002, 0003, or 0004 would be winners. A card that says 0079, for example, would be a loser. Bitcoin began with a difficulty level that Satoshi described as "ridiculously easy," meaning to win new coins at the beginning of bitcoin's existence, miners wouldn't have to employ much computing power. In the first year of bitcoin, only a few billion hashes were needed to generate blocks, which sounds like a lot but could be accomplished on any average laptop running the bitcoin software in the background of other tasks. This "ridiculously easy" difficulty level, however, didn't last as competition joined the network. In bitcoin, the difficulty target *adjusts*.

What happens when more competition arrives to generate blocks? If more miners try to generate blocks, the odds suggest that valid blocks will appear more quickly, resulting in a faster introduction of new coins. To counter this, Satoshi pioneered an automatic adjustment.

*It'll get a lot harder when competition makes the **automatic adjustment drive up the difficulty**.*

Herein lies one of the magic ingredients that helps secure the bitcoin network. Bitcoin's difficulty and target move inversely to each other: an automatic adjustment that drives difficulty higher means a target that gets smaller, which means more leading zeros. The bitcoin protocol measures the speed at which blocks are generated over a two-week period—2,016 blocks, which, at an *average* of 10 minutes per block, is 14 days. As of this writing, bitcoin's difficulty has increased about 400 times out of 439 total adjustments in its lifespan, moving bitcoin mining activity from laptops, to dedicated hardware by 2012, to the gargantuan server farms belonging to publicly traded bitcoin mining corporations today.

Bitcoin blocks don't appear exactly every 10 minutes— that is only the average. Some blocks arrive within a few minutes of each other, while others can take up to an hour. Because bitcoin miners engage in a game of chance when performing hashes, there is no guarantee a block will be found every 10 minutes. When blocks appear every eight minutes on average, for example, bitcoin's difficulty automatically adjusts to make finding a valid hash *more difficult* by setting a *smaller target*. This should theoretically slow the creation of blocks until more miners join the network. If miners leave the network, blocks appear more slowly, and the network's difficulty will adjust to make it easier for miners.

Bitcoin's seemingly slow settlement process of sometimes up to an hour before transactions are considered safe to mark as settled helps to protect individual nodes from fraud. It isn't practical for a café to wait 30 minutes for payments to settle before serving coffee, but a manufacturer in China is happy to wait an hour to verify the bitcoin blockchain after receiving a large payment before shipping goods to Brazil. There is no central authority in bitcoin for the Chinese company to ask if the Brazilians are sending real money. All that is needed is a bitcoin node, which downloads blocks one at a time from the network. And while bitcoin mining is a computationally intensive process that requires specialized machinery, running a basic bitcoin node to keep individual oversight over the bitcoin blockchain is not. Operating a bitcoin node is feasible on any modern laptop—Satoshi clearly designed the bitcoin protocol with open access and low barriers to entry in mind. If bitcoin required expensive computing hardware just to verify balances, it wouldn't be a viable solution to centralized finance.

Bitcoin Protocol Rule #6: Open access

Satoshi described a network available to the masses in his original paper:

> *The network itself requires minimal structure. Messages are broadcast on a best effort basis, and nodes can leave and rejoin the network at will, accepting the longest proof-of-work chain as proof of what happened while they were gone.*[51]

With his code announcement, Satoshi also explained how offline functionality was built into the protocol:

---

51 *Nakamoto, "Bitcoin: A Peer-to-Peer Electronic Cash System."*

*If the recipient is not online, it is possible to send to their Bitcoin address, which is a hash of their **public key** that they give you. They'll receive the **transaction** the next time they connect and get the block it's in.*[52]

For security, people do not need to go online to generate a private key or even its corresponding address—anybody can generate a bitcoin private key and address in an offline environment and share *only* the address with others, preventing private keys from ever touching the internet. Digital signatures can also be completed in offline environments before transactions are broadcast online. Friendliness to offline participants is another way Satoshi opened access to bitcoin's protocol so that truly anybody can become a secure user.

Bitcoin Protocol Rule #7: ฿21,000,000

The final sprinkle of magic that ties bitcoin's rules together is its supply schedule—an intentional contrast to the dollar, which expands at a rate of at least 7% per year. Unofficially, however, the dollar's true growth rate is unmeasurable—despite efforts from the BIS to enact the Basel Accords, statistics on Eurodollars and currency derivatives are nearly impossible to compile. For bitcoin, the exact supply of coins over its entire lifespan is outlined in Satoshi's original code announcement, a mathematical precision strike at the heart of a banking system which expands at an unknowable rate. Satoshi created digital scarcity:

---

52 *Nakamoto, "Bitcoin v0.1 Released," 8 Jan 2009.*

*Total **circulation will be 21,000,000 coins**. It'll be distributed to network nodes when they make blocks, with the amount cut in half every 4 years.*

first 4 years: 10,500,000 coins
next 4 years: 5,250,000 coins
next 4 years: 2,625,000 coins
next 4 years: 1,312,500 coins
etc...

*When that runs out, the system can support transaction fees if needed. It's based on **open market competition**, and there will probably always be nodes willing to process transactions for free.*

Satoshi Nakamoto

We might never know the reasoning behind Satoshi's decision around the rules of bitcoin's supply, but in hindsight, we can only marvel at the incentive structure he created. Decentralized electronic cash had never before existed, so the first successful attempt needed to have rules that would make it attractive to others. Bitcoin didn't have investors or anybody to financially pull the project along—adoption would need to come from word-of-mouth endorsements based on a belief that it worked. A maximum of 21 million coins deeply resonated with cypherpunks, who were well versed in monetary history and the penchant of leaders to print money.

Satoshi decided on four-year events that we now call *halvings*, named because the mining reward halves itself between one block and the next. A four-year period at

10-minute blocks comes out to approximately 210,000 blocks—Satoshi's writings show he might have chosen this period deliberately to muster up market cycles of greed and fear which can bootstrap adoption. To illustrate halvings, from the start of bitcoin until block 210,000, each miner that generated a block earned ฿50, at which point ฿10.5 million had entered circulation. Then, the miner of block 210,001 earned ฿25 after the first halving event took place in 2012. As of this writing, block 886,688, miners earn ฿3.125 per block, and over ฿19.8 million bitcoin are in circulation—about 94% of the total ฿21,000,000.

When the first halving occurred in 2012 exactly as Satoshi intended, the small world of bitcoin users celebrated it as the moment the network officially observed and respected the rules of its strict supply algorithm. Halving events are each a grand testament to the decentralization of bitcoin because they show us nobody can change the supply rules—they recurred in 2016, 2020, and 2024. By 2040, the amount of new bitcoin awarded to the miner of each block will be less than ฿0.2, at which point over 99.8% of all bitcoin will already be in circulation. Bitcoin's embedded scarcity has bootstrapped its growth—users want to own something both rare and mathematically secure, and they like knowing it only gets more difficult to capture new coins because each block generated leaves a smaller portion of bitcoin unmined. The fight over ฿21 million is underway, as the world competes over *digital gold*.

Part of bitcoin's success must be attributed to Satoshi's planning mastery, as if he deeply understood human behavior and originated protocol features that would make people gravitate to bitcoin over a longer time frame. One of those features helps attract miners even without earning new coins. They can also earn transaction fees: because a limited number of transactions fit into each block, senders attach a fee to their transactions as an incentive for miners to add them to the blockchain. Bitcoin's blocks are vessels, and sometimes they can be very expensive to use based on surrounding demand.

By combining ₿21,000,000 (Rule #7) with the difficulty adjustment (Rule #5), Satoshi broke conventional economics by eliminating the classical theory of supply response—also known as supply elasticity.

Imagine a farmer that produces two agricultural crops—corn and strawberries. He plants half of the area with corn and the other half with strawberries. He then decides to split his efforts between the two crops because the amount he can earn from each is similar. One season, however, the strawberry bushes from his neighboring state don't produce fruit because of harsh weather, devastating the surrounding strawberry industry. Lack of supply drives prices up, and the higher prices cause our farmer to plant all strawberries and no corn the following season. Market prices eventually come down after he and others produce more strawberries to meet demand. This concept of higher prices drawing out more supply is consistent in every corner of the economy—scarcity increases prices, which motivates producers to make more, which helps bring prices back down.

In the bitcoin economy, if prices go up and more miners join the network to generate blocks, the difficulty to generate blocks increases and prevents them from being generated more quickly. That would be like if, after strawberry prices spiked and more farmers planted strawberries, all strawberry bushes grew slower. With no supply response after price increases thanks to automatic difficulty adjustments, the price of bitcoin isn't driven lower by a flurry of miners generating blocks and flooding the market with new coins. The bitcoin price fluctuates as network participants and speculators buy and sell, but its fixed and automatically adjusting supply schedule can't be compared to anything else in economics, from goods to labor to even gold. Higher prices *always* bring new supply onto the market, no matter what good or service we consider—*except for bitcoin.*

Bitcoin's scarcity sits on the other end of the spectrum from the continuously expanding credit system. The fixed supply of ₿21 million becomes exceedingly incongruent with $1 quadrillion in credit and currency derivatives, a dichotomy that causes prices in dollars and prices in bitcoin to move in opposite directions. In dollars, prices appear to be going up forever; in bitcoin terms, they are constantly going down.

* * *

With no coins, no transactions to process, and only one node in the network, Satoshi generated the first block without anybody else watching. That didn't stop him from placing an encoded message in place of bitcoin transactions. On January 3, 2009, Satoshi Nakamoto generated the first bitcoin block, also known as the "Genesis Block," embedding this headline from the UK-based newspaper *The Times*:

> *The Times 03/Jan/2009 Chancellor on brink of second bailout for banks*

It is our understanding that whoever Satoshi Nakamoto was, the pseudonym had explicitly invented an alternative to credit-system dominance—his mention of bank bailouts in the embedded message is the smoking gun. In Satoshi's subsequent public writings during bitcoin's early years, we learn that his motivations to create bitcoin derived from frustrations with a currency and banking deposit supply that lacked protocol boundaries altogether:

> *The root problem with conventional currency is all the trust that's required to make it work. The central bank must be trusted not to debase the currency, but the history of fiat currencies is full of breaches of that trust. Banks must be trusted to hold our money and transfer it electronically, but they lend it out in waves of credit bubbles with barely a fraction in reserve.*[53]

Almost instantly, bitcoin amassed a following of believers who recognized it as a solution to the global banking

---

53   Nakamoto, "Bitcoin: Open Source," 11 Feb 2009.

dollar and credit-system dominance. These early adopters started to save in a protocol-based money backed not by governments, banks, or gold, but by cryptography and ingenious game theory.

CHAPTER 11

LIFTOFF

"I just want to report that I successfully traded 10,000
bitcoins for pizza."
-LASZLO HANYECZ, May 22, 2010

HUMANS INVENTED OVAL-SHAPED STONES ALMOST 2 MILLION years ago—carefully carved by hand, these tools helped early nomads forage, build, and most importantly, kill prey. Archeologists believe these tools allowed our species to live in new areas and ascend the food chain. Money is also a tool—although it doesn't directly help humans consume food by contributing to the hunting process, money is a technology that helps us to trade, which encourages people to specialize and become more productive. In its ideal form, money can be an avenue to peaceful collaboration if it is *widely accepted and predictable.*

Today, the dollar is universally accepted as money, but its credit-based origin leads to a pervasive borrowing culture that punishes a saver's mentality. Cost-of-living increases often dwarf income growth, a dynamic unlikely to change from within. Banks will never establish a protocol with supply limits because there are too many stakeholders unwilling to relinquish their power to create credits. Even with Basel-based capital requirements, bankers possess an innate ability to skirt regulations by creating new varieties of financial derivatives. Dollars begin losing value the instant they are earned because they are constantly being diluted from several angles at once—banks create money when they lend to private enterprises and central banks create high-powered money any time lending in the economy starts to contract. We live under a doctrine that perpetuates rising prices through the credit creation machine.

During the Great Depression of the 1930s, gold's anchor on central bank reserves was mandated by law via how much gold must be held in reserve against dollars created by the Federal Reserve. The gold coverage ratio limited credit creation and prolonged a period of deflation, wherein prices fell, borrowers defaulted, banks failed, and the economy mightily struggled. Gold took the brunt of the blame, leading to President Roosevelt's actions banning the ownership of gold in 1933 and President Nixon's gold shock in 1971 which ended the link once and for all. Without gold, the dollar became more accommodative but much less predictable. We argue that instead of religiously following a doctrine taken from the global economy's failed experience with a fractional credit system tied to gold a century ago, we should acknowledge that the alternative to a gold-linked dollar ended up hurting people by doubling the home price to income ratio.

Bitcoin was created with explicit predictability, with the idea being that wide acceptance would follow only if the network caught on. Bitcoin doesn't replace the credit system—it offers the opposite: non-credit money. It cannot be created by anybody. Its supply is known, increasing today by less than 1% per year, and at a declining rate. The disparity between bitcoin's predictability and the credit system's immeasurability best illustrates the difference between money and credit-money.

We can theorize on the difference between bitcoin and the global banking dollar, or we can run the numbers, starting when bitcoin hit $1 in February 2011. At that time, the median price of a home in the United States was both $150,000 and ₿150,000—in fact, the value of the entire bitcoin network was so small, only a dozen homes could be purchased with its entire market capitalization. We can start to see the power of bitcoin by 2015 when the dollar-price of a home had doubled, but the price of bitcoin increased by so much that it drove the bitcoin-price of a home nosediving from ₿150,000 to ₿1,000. It didn't stop there.

By the beginning of 2020, the median price of a home had increased to $400,000 while bitcoin reached $10,000, sending home prices tumbling yet again for those saving in the new technology—to ₿40. As of 2025, with homes at $420,000 but with a bitcoin price around $100,000, it would take *less than ₿5 to purchase one home.*

From ₿1,000 in 2015 to only ₿5 today, prices denominated in bitcoin have decreased by a staggering amount over the last decade. It's true that on its way from $1 to $100,000, bitcoin's price experienced enormous ups and downs, but we attribute such volatility to the traditional financial system's violent digestion of a new asset so disruptive that many of its holders believe it to be priceless while they wade through a sea of disbelievers.

Because bitcoin is a new form of money—lacking the physical allure of gold, the legal backing of government currency, or the extensibility of bank credit—its classification as an asset remains unclear. The label cryptocurrency fails to capture its true essence as money. Instead, bitcoin offers society a tool for saving that makes life more affordable without requiring individuals to chase the next risky investment. Patience has rewarded those who steadfastly hold through rough waves of volatility, as bitcoin's dollar-price has taken a roller-coaster ride to reach its market value today. Pierre Rochard, a researcher writing about bitcoin since 2012, aptly calls bitcoin the world's best *savings technology.*

Over the final four chapters, we'll detail how bitcoin went from an idea to an asset with market value, how it journeyed to $100,000 thanks to global adoption and a steady legitimization by the United States government, and why it will rise to $1 million and beyond over the coming years as it integrates with the modern credit system.

* * *

We begin bitcoin's price voyage in 2010 before ₿1 could even warrant $0.01 on any exchange. Laszlo Hanyecz worked a day job as a software developer in Florida, but in bitcoin's infancy, he started moonlighting as a miner, creatively tinkering with hardware and software to generate blocks more effectively than his network peers. During bitcoin's early months, network participants could mine bitcoin simply using their computers and CPU processing. Laszlo, who went by his first name on the bitcoin online forum bitcointalk.org, used faster graphics processors, or GPUs, to outcompete other bitcoin miners. His success in discovering the advantages of using the fastest chips available landed him thousands of coins. In May 2010, Laszlo posted an online request that helps us understand the process of how bitcoin first achieved adoption long before it traded 24 hours a day on cryptocurrency exchanges.

I'll pay 10,000 bitcoins for a couple of pizzas, like maybe 2 large ones so I have some left over for the next day...If you're interested please let me know and we can work out a deal.

Thanks,

Laszlo

A reply came through pointing out that Laszlo was probably overpaying for the $25 pizza order by helping him see the current market value of his proposal, "10,000... That's quite a bit.... you could sell those on *https://www.bitcoin-market.com/* for $41 right now." Laszlo could have sold the coins for dollars, but his goal wasn't to make money at that moment—he explained: "I just think it would be interesting if I could say that I paid for a pizza in bitcoins."

After he posted pictures of the successful food delivery, a fellow forum member congratulated him on the milestone of spending bitcoin in a real-world transaction and chronicling it for others. There is no way Laszlo could have known that the ฿10,000 he spent on pizza in 2010 would be worth $1 billion only 15 years later.[54]

* * *

People often wonder where bitcoin gets its value. Simply put, it comes from a collective belief in its properties and durability, a belief that had to start somewhere. In bitcoin's early years, its value was harder to see, especially when each coin was valued at less than one cent. A minuscule price failed to demonstrate any real-world monetary value, which also contributed to a low profile. That started to change with more eyeballs. Slashdot, one of the most frequented websites for coverage on the latest in technology development during the rise of the internet, described itself as "News for Nerds." Bitcoin's first publicity on Slashdot was in July 2010: a short article explaining the advent of a new digital cash gaining in popularity, which sent the price of bitcoin to $0.08. But with the Slashdot article bringing thousands of fresh eyes to Satoshi's idea, bitcoin experienced its first genuine opportunity to audition its protocol for practicality and interest.

It succeeded. A slew of critical thinkers, technology enthusiasts, and software developers seemed enthralled by

---

54 Namcios, "Bitcoin Pizza Day," Bitcoin Magazine.

the ideas and game theory at play, a process that we see replicate each time new people learn about Satoshi's creation. If we are to boil down bitcoin's success and adoption, it's that the ideas that underpin bitcoin are executed by its software and function exactly as advertised—electronic cash without banks.

Both gold and silver served as money for thousands of years on every continent out of a belief in the value of each. Nobody told human beings that gold is more valuable than silver, but societies and markets always priced it as such. Laszlo didn't need to convince somebody to accept ฿10,000 in exchange for about $25 in pizza; there was somebody who already believed the trade was worth it. Bitcoin is money because people have a belief that the unit, which is scarce and finite, will hold its value.

But bitcoin wasn't some perfect money from the start. Just a few weeks after the first Slashdot bitcoin article, a bug was discovered in the bitcoin software that allowed for somebody to create ฿184 billion in block 74,638. The overflow bug could have killed the young network protocol.

Satoshi rushed to provide an update but couldn't force everyone to switch over to a different blockchain without the buggy block—the network had too many people. One user pointed out, "I'm afraid the community is just too big and distributed now to expect much in the way of voluntary quick action on anything, especially generation which I'm sure many have on automatic and largely unmoderated."[55]

---

55   kencausey, "Re: Overflow bug SERIOUS."

The user was right. Satoshi's code became exposed to its first potentially catastrophic error, and the aura around the mysterious creator started to dissipate. For several hours, bitcoin's network experienced a crisis in functionality. The small community eventually reverted to the blockchain before the ฿184 billion buggy transaction, but confidence in Satoshi had waned. It was finally apparent that he wasn't perfect, and the community, at least mentally, still depended too much on Satoshi. Ironically, the necessity of Satoshi eventually leaving bitcoin's sphere to ensure its decentralization crept into the collective psyche. The founder must leave.

The beginning of the end had come for Satoshi Nakamoto, who completely stopped posting on the forums after bitcoin started to receive attention in conversations surrounding WikiLeaks. A long-time cypherpunk mailing list participant, Julian Assange, started a whistleblowing operation in quest of exposing government corruption around the world, and encryption tools enabled whistleblowers to protect their identities. Phil Zimmermann and Hal Finney contributed as much to WikiLeaks as Assange with their work on PGP encryption, which was mandatory in communications with the organization after less sophisticated methods left whistleblowers exposed.

Assange embodied the cypherpunk mentality. In 2006, he spearheaded WikiLeaks, a website dedicated to publishing secret documents exposing governments and intelligence agencies and their activities—whether illegal, brazen, or both. WikiLeaks exemplifies today's power dynamics, wherein individuals face mighty incumbents and seek to expose wrongdoing at an institutional level. The combination of brave whistleblowing, online encryption, and a cypherpunk leader helped the world to inspect the nature of today's corruption, bringing a desire for increased political transparency. After WikiLeaks released a slew of official US war logs from Afghanistan and Iraq, Visa, Mastercard, and PayPal blocked donations to the whistleblowing website. Suddenly, the world's only decentralized money, in which transactions couldn't be blocked by gatekeepers, popped into the conversation.

Technology magazine *PC World* published an article about bitcoin on its website titled "Could the WikiLeaks Scandal Lead to New Virtual Currency?", the largest press Satoshi's project had ever received and its second viral moment—substantially larger than the audience it received after the first Slashdot article. Satoshi did not share the enthusiasm of others at bitcoin's next round of attention.

From: satoshi
Subject: Re: PC World Article on Bitcoin
Date: December 11, 2010 at 23:39:16 UTC
It would have been nice to get this attention in any other context. WikiLeaks has kicked the hornet's nest, and the swarm is headed towards us.[56]

---

56 *Satoshi Nakamoto, "Re: PC World Article."*

The next day, as if spooked by the sudden fame and external scrutiny, Satoshi made his final post and vanished from the forums forever. He clearly wanted bitcoin to grow much more slowly versus being thrown into an intelligence battle. It was time to exit—a necessary step toward the proper decentralization of the bitcoin network.

Combining the programming mishaps, mass media attention, and the fact that the community was ready to be leaderless, Satoshi stepped aside at arguably the perfect time in bitcoin's young life. With plenty of deftly skilled cryptographers and software developers involved in bitcoin's software maintenance, his presence was no longer essential to the network. Subsequent press launched the price of bitcoin to $1— the rocket ship had officially taken flight. As bitcoin entered its post-creator era, it was clear that the founder going away was *good* for its trajectory.

CHAPTER 12

HIGH-POWERED MONEY

"It might make sense just to get some in case it catches on. If enough people think the same way, that becomes a self-fulfilling prophecy."[57]

-SATOSHI NAKAMOTO, January 16, 2009

I N THE 14 YEARS SINCE SATOSHI DISAPPEARED, BITCOIN'S price has risen from $1 to $100,000 as the world scrambles to understand why bitcoin has amassed more value, $2 trillion, than practically every individual company in the world. The answer is that people *value* bitcoin because, for the first time ever, it gives them access to *real money*. We must then ask, what is it precisely that makes people want it, and *why* is it valuable?

One of the most common misconceptions and doubts about bitcoin surrounds its *intrinsic* value. Intrinsic is a word to describe the usefulness of something—for example, people believe gold has intrinsic value not just because it's used in spaceships and jewelry, but also because it carries thousands of years of cultural appreciation. Gold has intrinsic value largely because of *perception*. Bitcoin is a purely digital construct, made entirely of ones and zeroes. In that

---

57   Satoshi Nakamoto, *"Bitcoin v0.1 Released,"* 16 Jan 2009.

vein, many people think bitcoin doesn't represent anything inherent—only speculation. But this description of bitcoin entirely fails to capture bitcoin's intrinsic value.

Bitcoin's value doesn't solely come from its qualities—it comes from *people who value those qualities*. People's preferences tell us what has value, and we must use price as our best measure of it. A painting by Pablo Picasso sold for over $100 million in 2015, while his sketches can sometimes be snagged in auction for a relatively paltry $5,000. What makes one painting so valuable but a pencil sketch less so? If it's a matter of color versus pencil, then why do some of Picasso's sketches sell for more money than his finished paintings? Art is a perfect example of the idea that *value is entirely subjective*, and the only thing that gives a Picasso painting, precious jewel, or bitcoin value is demand—people who desire those things. With demand comes market value and a price—the same qualities that brought bitcoin from $0 to $1 in 2011 mirror those destined to send it to $1 million per coin and beyond. Bitcoin's demand—why people covet it—is built on *three core principles:* decentralization, digital property, and scarcity.

* * *

Bitcoin's foundation is its software protocol—a network open to join, with software code available to all, held together by a steady cryptographic construction. In its early months, nobody had assigned any value to bitcoin yet. Then, slowly, people like Laszlo started to test whether bitcoin could work as money by using it in real-life transactions, such as swapping bitcoin for food delivery or a miner selling bitcoin to cover its equipment and electricity costs. The fact that bitcoin didn't have an issuer—no company making decisions, no CEO, and no central authority—wasn't lost on early adopters who were drawn to bitcoin after witnessing the system's game theory in action. These earliest adopters saw bitcoin's value as money without a center—the *first principle* of bitcoin demand is its *decentralization*.

Bitcoin's blockchain is a string of transaction data, and because that data exists everywhere a bitcoin node exists, the network is now embedded into the internet. Without shutting down internet infrastructure, there is no way to turn bitcoin off. Bitcoin does not have a corporate entity, an executive in charge, or server farms operating in dedicated locations. Instead, bitcoin's open source code, relatively low bandwidth, and online network allow anybody to join as a participant with equal rights within the software. Importantly for bitcoin, the difficulty of generating blocks increases over time as the network grows, making it challenging for any one participant to gain outsized control over the processing of transactions. In this way, if a bitcoin owner wishes to send a transaction, there is no way for any one participant to prevent that transaction from entering the blockchain. Once it's added, it becomes irreversible for all nodes to see. When quantum computing arrives, bitcoin's protocol will rely on those who write the best software code to integrate quantum-level encryption and maintain decentralization.

Bitcoin nodes started popping up all over the world after Satoshi launched the software. Martti Malmi, a student from Finland, was one of the first programmers to ever contact Satoshi directly—within four months of the first block in 2009, he had offered to improve bitcoin's source code. Early bitcoin users appeared in the UK and Germany during the first year of bitcoin, with mining nodes in China's Sichuan province joining the network by stationing facilities next to readily available and cheap hydroelectric power. One user at a time, one country at a time, small communities began to form. Enthusiasts helped grow adoption by starting bitcoin businesses, spreading gospel about the benefits of decentralized cash, and bringing access to locals. Many started adopting bitcoin before the first US regulatory rulings labeled it a "virtual currency" in 2013, so although we argue the immense influence of the US government on bitcoin's legitimization in the next chapter, we can see bitcoin *usage* in every corner of the world map during its first five years. Part of what makes bitcoin decentralized is its global reach—out of 195 countries in the world, over 130 have bitcoin nodes today, and over 60 have nodes that are competitively mining.

In Argentina, bitcoin shined as an alternative to government currency as early as 2011. Capital controls prevented the exchange of local currency for US dollars, boosting the black market for US currency, and before long, bitcoin. Peer-to-peer exchanges became popular in Buenos Aires, as bitcoin took on a new protective role for victims of government mismanagement, money printing, and rampant inflation. By

2012, bitcoin meetups were happening around the city, the first bar started accepting bitcoin as payment for drinks, and people found digital shelter from currency devaluation.

Expatriates from the Philippines scatter the world across the health care, maritime shipping, and hospitality industries—over 2 million people are estimated to remit over $30 billion annually back to family members in their home country. For years, Western Union held monopolistic power over the flow of money from overseas back to the country, but from 2014, companies helped reduce remittance fees charged to these Filipino families from 8% to 3% by using bitcoin.

Savings were even larger in Kenya, where BitPesa became the first regulated bitcoin company in Africa—the company helped Kenyans working in the UK reduce remittance fees from over 10% to 3%. Nigeria and South Africa both hosted early bitcoin exchanges to help people in those nations achieve better financial services and avoid currency devaluation. People in each of these countries found value in bitcoin because it helped them *solve problems.*

With nodes all over the world, bitcoin lacked a geographic center and, as an online network, physical jurisdiction. By designing a network of equal nodes, Satoshi invented money *without a state.* We explained how financial institutions create most of the credits circulating today as currency, but those credits wouldn't have legitimacy without their association to the US government and support of the Federal Reserve. With bitcoin, much like is the case with precious metals, money can circulate without the stamp of a nation or the assistance of banks. Decentralized money implies both the freedom to transact and a shift toward self-reliance. Bitcoin has started a monetary trend of people choosing cryptographic systems over the financial industry, and self-custody over gatekeeping.

* * *

The word 'cryptocurrency' is short for the term 'cryptographic currency.' Bitcoin employs cryptographic functions, but we argue that *currency* is far from its most appropriate descriptor. Currency today describes a form of money that circulates—the word comes from the Latin verb *currere*, meaning 'to run' or 'to flow.' Bitcoin flows to and from different users every time a new block is confirmed, creating a current—by that definition, is bitcoin a currency? Yes, because the network's blockchain architecture enables the circulation of money by processing transactions. But bitcoin is *much more* than a *transactional* currency. In late 2010, Hal Finney envisioned bitcoin not as a currency for day-to-day transactions, but as a *reserve currency* and *high-powered money*:

> *I believe this will be the ultimate fate of Bitcoin, to be the "high-powered money" that serves as a reserve currency for banks that issue their own digital cash. Most Bitcoin transactions will occur between banks, to settle net transfers. Bitcoin transactions by private individuals will be as rare as... well, as Bitcoin based purchases are today.*[58]

---

58 Hal Finney, "Re: Bitcoin Bank," 30 Dec 2010.

Finney explained that bitcoin can be used as reserves— money for interbank settlement—as well as the collateral basis for the creation for more dollar-credits. But even "high-powered money" as a term fails to encapsulate bitcoin's range as an asset. The *second principle* of bitcoin demand stems from its qualities as *digital property*.

Bitcoin has achieved a network effect by excelling as the perfect form of private property in the digital world. Property rights empower decision-making, investment in long-term projects, and promote innovation to improve the quality of the property and capabilities of its performance. Judicial precedent for property rights sponsors business formation and capital markets: with legal protection for equity holders, those with capital can pool interests to pursue large economic endeavors that would be impossible without a joint effort protected by the law. Bitcoin achieves property rights digitally.

Bitcoin provides an alternative to each asset class by doing something that others cannot—starting with how it allows a person to take full ownership so quickly from anywhere without paperwork or custodians. For real estate, bitcoin offers a substitute to physical property. Buildings have high maintenance costs and localized risk—a city could lose economic viability relative to another, for example. Property ownership is a legal construct because property deeds change hands through the government, and owning real estate in a foreign country often requires registration and paying excess taxes. Equities operate similarly—the ownership itself is conducted through brokerages and custodians, and subject to registration or taxes levied by governments. Owning bitcoin bypasses financial institutions and even the very idea of an asset's durability—bitcoin doesn't decay like a building without maintenance, can't lose profitability like a company being outcompeted, and if we learn our lesson from the internet's evolution, will not be replaced by another protocol for electronic cash.

*   *   *

Peter Carl Fabergé inherited his father's jewelry business in 1882 and elevated the Russian brand to a globally recognized designer of luxury decorated art. Fifty ornate jeweled eggs were commissioned by Russian Czars Alexander III and Nicholas II, designed by Fabergé in Saint Petersburg and distributed to the royal family over the course of 22 years. These eggs, most of which are now held in museums or private art collections, are worth millions of dollars each, have intrinsic value because they are made from precious metals, and are extremely rare. Yet nobody would consider a Fabergé egg a form of money just because of these qualities.

Bitcoin circulates as money online, isn't constrained by physical nature or divisibility, and is strictly limited to 21 million coins in total supply—a quantity never to be exceeded. Credits, on the other hand, are predestined to lose purchasing power in a chaotic world, and therefore avoiding the dilution of credits can be elusive. Thankfully, bitcoin offers us a shielding tool that can help people improve their lives. Bitcoin nodes allow anyone to participate in a network with rules that are open, unchanging, and impossible for any one participant to manipulate. The public doesn't trust the global banking dollar or any other national currency to protect their earnings and savings, which forces people to invest in stocks and real estate to outpace cost-of-living increases. Another traditional way to avoid credits is gold, but gold cannot be transferred via fiberoptic undersea cables and satellite transmissions to the most remote parts of the planet like bitcoin can. It cannot be subdivided without melting the metal, while bitcoin transactions can be sent in amounts as low as ₿0.00000001. It cannot be stored in one's brain like the 12-word seed phrases powering bitcoin wallets that convert private keys into a secure yet simple string of English words.

When people earn dollars, whether paid in cash or direct deposit into their checking account, they collect bank deposits that can easily be duplicated by bank loan application approvals, the sway of an election, or a politician's executive action amid a crisis-induced opportunity. Bitcoin, on the other hand, contains a ruleset that explicitly prohibits discretionary expansion, guarding those who earn bitcoin against unwanted dilution. Its wild price swings in dollar terms have unfortunately disallowed many seeking immediate gratification from experiencing the impact that bitcoin can have on their lives—saving in bitcoin dramatically reduces the cost of living.

From the original laptop bitcoin miners scattered around the world, to those evading capital controls, to anybody simply seeking an escape from the dilution of credit-money, there are hundreds of millions of people around the world who have switched their savings over to bitcoin because they believe it is *better money*. While the decentralization and cryptographically enforced property rights of bitcoin brought it early attention and adoption, its diametrical opposition to the credit system, wherein credit expands at least 7% per year but bitcoin's increases are flattening out, is the glue that holds bitcoin together. Bitcoin's *scarcity*, our *third core principle*, is bitcoin's ultimate game theory—Satoshi created an asset that was specifically designed to go up in price. Only six weeks after his first software release in 2009, he described bitcoin's supply limit as gold-like, contrasted it to the elasticity of credit, and predicted the overall demand for digital scarcity we have witnessed for the past 16 years:

> *In this sense, it's more typical of a precious metal. Instead of the supply changing to keep the value the same, the supply is predetermined and the value changes. As the number of users grows, the value per coin increases. It has the potential for a positive feedback loop; as users increase, the value goes up, which could attract more users to take advantage of the increasing value.*[59]

An online protocol for money changes the way our species interacts with one another, but it also exposes the nature of credit-money, its dependence on ever-increasing amounts

---

59 Nakamoto, "Bitcoin: Open Source," 18 Feb 2009.

of borrowing, and banking influence over our time and labor. The *decentralization, property rights, and scarcity* of bitcoin can liberate people from the credit system by allowing them to keep the fruits of their labor. We're reminded of why the hovering mechanic from Star Wars refused credits from the Galactic Republic, and we're left wondering if bitcoin would have sufficed as payment.

CHAPTER 13

UNITED STATES OF BITCOIN

"Every day that goes by and Bitcoin hasn't collapsed due to legal or technical problems, that brings new information to the market. It increases the chance of Bitcoin's eventual success and justifies a higher price."[60]

-HAL FINNEY, June 4, 2011

U NCERTAINTY SURROUNDING BITCOIN'S FUTURE TORmented its price in 2011, crashing from its $30 peak to below $3. Infamous online marketplace Silk Road founder Ross Ulbricht recognized the value of an online currency that couldn't be blocked or restricted, employing bitcoin from the website's inception to help buyers and sellers connect anonymously. Bitcoin helped the Silk Road's users avoid banks and skirt US regulations, drawing the ire of US Senate members in June 2011 and eventually a long prosecution involving the Justice Department and FBI—Ulbricht, one of the strongest early bitcoin champions, received a Presidential pardon in 2025 after serving a decade in prison for his online crimes.

---

60   Hal Finney, *"Re: Bitcoin and the Efficient Market Hypothesis."*

Subsequent price volatility elicited prominent economists and bankers to denounce bitcoin as a currency, spooking the public from identifying it as more than a currency used in illicit trade.

But not everybody got scared away—American technologists expressed their interest in bitcoin, and despite a rocky relationship with the nascent technology, the US government eventually started to come around, one financial regulator and lawmaker at a time. When considering the legacy of J.C.R. Licklider's vision of an Intergalactic Computer Network, how the US government sponsored the internet's creation, and how the NSA lost to the public in the crypto war, the country seemed destined to ultimately accept bitcoin's role as a *savings and freedom technology*—even if it would take several years. When Daniel Bernstein won his case against the State Department, the courts protected cryptography under the First Amendment and unknowingly set a crucial precedent for bitcoin years before its birth.

Because bitcoin's design offers an *alternative* to government-issued currency, reduces reliance on banks, and allows participants to self-verify the authenticity of transactions, many wrongly assume the United States government would default to restrictive or prohibitive policies. This couldn't be further from the truth—despite bitcoin's complicated relationship with certain factions within the US government over the network's lifespan, the United States of America and its judiciary have come to exert a *strong influence* on the adoption of bitcoin as a monetary network.

The term "S-curve adoption" describes how people adopt new technologies—the curve itself looks like the letter S—starting slowly, then going almost vertically, then flattening out at the end. At first, a small group of early enthusiasts gently builds into a community with its first tools. Once enough of the early infrastructure is built, the next wave of people increases the liveliness of the network, and only then can a technology achieve mass adoption. Later in its life cycle, a technology's adoption rate flattens out as most people have already joined—much like where the internet sits in its S-curve today. Along with the internet, this pattern repeated with the adoption of electricity grids, televisions, and smartphones, and can now be witnessed in bitcoin. The United States has a strong history of actively participating in the early stages of major S-curve adoption technologies and is perfectly positioned not to fight, but to embrace and study bitcoin to ensure the nation's healthy participation in a technology already engaged in the S-curve.

Price appreciation of bitcoin, buying and selling activity within American borders, and young technology companies building services around bitcoin are all attracting increased economic activity to the US relative to other, more skeptical, countries. Most importantly, bitcoin is a peer-to-peer technology that the US government can't block without criminalizing its use or shutting down the internet itself. We believe that because bitcoin exists as an open internet protocol—born in the echoes of ARPANET, shaped by the NSA's cryptography legacy, and informed by the US' historical experience with neutral money—an American acceptance of bitcoin comes naturally. A ban would have been challenged and defeated in the courts, as the State Department had already lost the Bernstein case on First Amendment grounds over code-as-speech, and the country has no obligation to prevent a separation of money and state that might occur due to technological progress given the legacy of precious metal in the US Constitution.

Finally, the country itself is designed as a decentralized operation—with three branches of government structured to balance each other, no individual or branch can seize control of the entire system. Its republican form of government—wherein power rests with the people, and the individual is protected—resembles the architecture of both the internet and bitcoin. US military and intelligence organizations have the most influence on the country's longer-term goals, and we see that in the military's creation of ARPANET, which demonstrated a forward-thinking approach to technology and networking its citizens and researchers. Those who worry about bitcoin being banned or restricted by the US government haven't been following along—the United States of America is the most pro-bitcoin nation in the world, not because its bitcoin-related laws are explicitly the friendliest, but because a free society that empowers the individual through republicanism, the internet, and bitcoin is enhanced by protecting the usage of all three. Parts of the government began recognizing this as early as 2013, marking the *first* of *five major public policy actions* taken by the United States to become the home of bitcoin.

* * *

How did the US government come to know about bitcoin? Gavin Andresen, Satoshi's early bitcoin collaborator, presented to the CIA about bitcoin in mid-2011, although we don't have any detail on how the agency responded. In addition to the CIA, the Drug Enforcement Agency had knowledge of the Silk Road around a similar timeframe because it was tracking narcotics trafficked on the website, while the FBI officially launched its Silk Road investigation by the end of that year. From the cryptography side, the NSA, which built the hash function used in bitcoin behind the Triple Fence, doesn't exactly document its surveillance but it's safe to assume the government's cryptographers had knowledge of bitcoin's launch and early uptake. Despite multiple federal agencies being tangentially aware of bitcoin and its ability to let users bypass the financial system, the first official ruling from the financial side of the government was positive. It provided a government-ascribed classification and definition—both sorely lacking at the time—and ignited the bitcoin market.

FinCEN, or Financial Crimes Enforcement Network, was established within the US Treasury Department in 1990 to provide the government with financial intelligence. The country's relationship with banking surveillance dates back to 1970, when the Bank Secrecy Act was passed into law, targeting organized crime's usage of banks. From that point on, escalating with FinCEN's involvement and the later expanded government surveillance powers from the Patriot Act in 2001, banks began operating—and continue to date—as a spy arm of the government, monitoring the bank dealings of its citizens and their credit card usage without warrants or pushback. In 1999, FinCEN put forth a classification called the Money Service Business (MSB) to identify the financial entities responsible for the collection of information from their customers and those who carry a legal obligation to report all suspicious activity directly to the Treasury Department.

When FinCEN ruled on cryptocurrency broadly in March 2013, the primary motivation was to declare cryptocurrency exchanges (companies that allowed customers to buy and sell bitcoin in exchange for US dollar deposits) as MSBs. All exchanges were from that point on required to register with FinCEN, which made them subject to reporting requirements of the Bank Secrecy Act. Most important was the official ruling that *bitcoin itself doesn't have a legally recognizable central authority* and that *bitcoin miners performing computations are not MSBs.* From the FinCEN ruling:

A final type of convertible virtual currency activity involves a de-centralized convertible virtual currency (1) that has no central repository and no single administrator, and (2) that persons may obtain by their own computing or manufacturing effort. A person that creates units of this convertible virtual currency and uses it to purchase real or virtual goods and services is a user of the convertible virtual currency and not subject to regulation as a money transmitter.[61]

---

61   *FinCEN, "Fin-2013-G001."*

This *first* of five monumental policy declarations from FinCEN might seem as only tacit approval, but with bitcoin in the crosshairs of the DEA and CIA and amid a multiyear Silk Road investigation during which the FBI seized over ₿100,000, the average bitcoin user and miner escaped without as much as even a slap on the wrist. This was the US government's first way of saying "Americans are allowed to own and mine bitcoin." In the weeks after the ruling, bitcoin quadrupled in price from $50 to $200, an admission from the market that it had not yet considered the reality of a pro-bitcoin US government regulatory stance.

About one year after the FinCEN ruling, the US government took its *second* policy advance toward legitimizing bitcoin when the IRS struck its tax ruling, classifying bitcoin as property and that sales are subject to capital gains—a similar tax treatment to gold coins or real estate. By recognizing the digital asset should be subject to capital gains, bitcoin achieved more legitimacy without its owners subject to any tax penalties or punitive restrictions. Both FinCEN and the IRS had the chance to institute guidance against bitcoin or recommend that legislators move toward more prohibitive action, but they didn't. With these two US rulings, bitcoin users, miners, and entrepreneurs could invest in the progress of bitcoin as a network without fear, building tools that allow people to use, store, spend, and financialize it more effectively.

The importance of the *third* US government policy action cannot be overstated. In 2016, the Chicago Mercantile

Exchange (CME), the world's largest futures exchange, launched a bitcoin price index to start officially tracking the bitcoin price, which at the time still fully relied on cryptocurrency exchanges with minimal ties to traditional New York and Chicago firms. For the CME to stay competitive, it knew that initiating the trading of bitcoin futures contracts was essential. For that, the CME would need permission from the Commodity Futures Trading Commission (CFTC), the relevant US regulator. To pave the way for bitcoin futures in 2015, the CFTC officially declared bitcoin a commodity:

> *In the Order, the CFTC for the first time finds that Bitcoin and other virtual currencies are properly defined as commodities.*[62]

By passing the CFTC test, bitcoin adoption could accelerate because futures contracts allow integration with, as opposed to a competition with, the credit system and its global banking dollar. We believe the *Bitcoin Age* began during this period because it's when bitcoin arrived on the doorstep of the existing financial system.

One of the biggest challenges to bitcoin adoption for the masses has always been investing in the asset itself. Without the technical skills to manage a bitcoin private key and take custody of coins, investors who wish to purchase bitcoin were left with few options. Using bitcoin as collateral in other financial dealings was nearly impossible. CME futures

---

62 *CME Group, "Announce Launch."*

contracts, however, forever changed the way that institutional investors could participate in bitcoin, all stemming from the CFTC decision. After the US government recognized bitcoin as digital gold, its price took its next leap higher, moving from $500 to $5,000 over the next year.

The *fourth* policy move from the US was the approval of bitcoin exchange-traded funds (ETFs) in 2024. Financial startup Grayscale's private bitcoin fund was the first traditional investment vehicle to gain early traction in US markets and at one point held over 3% of all bitcoin in circulation, but its fund was not a public security regulated by the US Securities and Exchange Commission (SEC). Grayscale's product was highly coveted because it gave investors a legal claim on bitcoin ownership without having to manage private seeds, seed phrases, or accounts with unregulated cryptocurrency exchanges. The fund manager, which for years tried to convert its private fund to an ETF security regulated by the SEC, was consistently met with opposition. Over several years, the SEC repeatedly denied Grayscale's ETF approval applications, causing Grayscale to sue the SEC for inconsistent treatment. Grayscale won its case in October 2023, when a federal judge ruled that the SEC was "arbitrary and capricious" in its ETF denial, an embarrassing defeat for the securities regulator. Once the SEC was shot down by the Justice Department, the regulator had no choice but to approve ETFs issued by Grayscale, megalithic asset managers BlackRock and Fidelity, and several others. In January 2024, ETFs went live. The floodgates had opened—now, investors could buy bitcoin in brokerage accounts traditionally purposed to purchase stocks, a pool of capital exceeding $100 trillion. The early demand for these products in the United States was jolting.

The introduction of BlackRock's and Fidelity's ETFs, specifically, brought an incumbent's legitimacy to bitcoin. A global banking dollar in perpetual devaluation had driven investors to gold in great quantities after enormous bank bailouts following the 2008 financial crisis, but BlackRock's bitcoin ETF passed its gold ETF in size *only months* after its release. Interest in bitcoin is so strong that the BlackRock bitcoin fund is already one of the world's largest ETFs and has grown *larger than any single ETF launched over the past 10 years*, making it the most successful ETF launch in history. Add in Fidelity's bitcoin ETF, and the two have already surpassed the leading gold ETF, managed by State Street. Thousands of the world's largest institutional investors have already begun stockpiling bitcoin assets, including the hedge fund giant Citadel, Abu Dhabi's $1-trillion sovereign wealth fund, and investment banking stalwart Goldman Sachs. Whatever negative stigma associated with bitcoin investment and cryptographic custody in its early years disappeared once and for all with the BlackRock and Fidelity ETFs—now, there was no excuse to have zero bitcoin allocation given its historic price performance and global popularity as a savings technology.

The *fifth* and final US policy move toward legitimizing bitcoin in the United States was the formation of a Strategic Bitcoin Reserve, creating a Digital Fort Knox—a strategic bitcoin stockpile to complement the country's gold holdings and prepare for our evolving monetary future. Signed by President Donald Trump in early 2025, the executive orders pivot the US government toward a full embrace of bitcoin and protect private bitcoin usage in the United States. The first order in January provided an example for the rest of the world to follow, that bitcoin is a technology worth protecting:

The digital asset industry plays a crucial role in innovation and economic development in the United States, as well as our Nation's international leadership. It is therefore the policy of my Administration to support the responsible growth and use of digital assets, blockchain technology, and related technologies across all sectors of the economy, including by protecting and promoting the ability of individual citizens and private-sector entities alike to access and use for lawful purposes open public blockchain networks without persecution, including the ability to develop and deploy software, to participate in mining and validating, to transact with other persons without unlawful censorship, and to maintain self-custody of digital assets.[63]

In March, the country officially established a Strategic Bitcoin Reserve to harness bitcoin's power. It explained its justification:

Bitcoin is the original cryptocurrency. The Bitcoin protocol permanently caps the total supply of bitcoin (BTC) at 21

---

63 *The White House, "Strengthening American Leadership."*

million coins, and has never been hacked. As a result of its scarcity and security, Bitcoin is often referred to as "digital gold". Because there is a fixed supply of BTC, there is a strategic advantage to being among the first nations to create a strategic bitcoin reserve. The United States Government currently holds a significant amount of BTC, but has not implemented a policy to maximize BTC's strategic position as a unique store of value in the global financial system. Just as it is in our country's interest to thoughtfully manage national ownership and control of any other resource, our Nation must harness, not limit, the power of digital assets for our prosperity.[64]

The pair of executive orders from the White House accurately captured Satoshi's creation of a public blockchain and proved that the US government had officially recognized the value of digital gold and the arrival of a *Bitcoin Age*. America's tradition of freedom, protection of the individual, a system of private property, and the prospect of economic opportunity blend together within bitcoin to embody the nation's greatest ideals.

---

64   *The White House, "Establishment of the Strategic Bitcoin Reserve."*

CHAPTER 14

BITCOIN AGE

"As an amusing thought experiment, imagine that Bitcoin is successful and becomes the dominant payment system in use throughout the world. Then the total value of the currency should be equal to the total value of all the wealth in the world. Current estimates of total worldwide household wealth that I have found range from $100 trillion to $300 trillion. With 20 million coins, that gives each coin a value of about $10 million." [65]

—HAL FINNEY, January 11, 2009

B ITCOIN IS CHANGING THE WORLD AS WE KNOW IT. IT SHIFTS the balance of power to individuals away from banks, offers freedom from credit-money, and transforms our relationship with electricity, which is required to sustain the network. Today, it is estimated that over 500 million people, or somewhere around 6% of the global population, own some amount of bitcoin. The protocol's 16-year growth trajectory has continued to closely follow that of the internet, email, smartphones, and social networks—technologies that all have billions of users but started with only a few, like Charley Kline at UCLA and Bill Duvall at Stanford for the first ARPANET

---

65   *Hal Finney, "Bitcoin v0.1 released."*

message, or Satoshi Nakamoto and Hal Finney for the first bitcoin transaction. These networks started not as sprawling webs, but between only two individuals. Function and belief led to the rest.

Bitcoin's largest impact comes from financially empowering the masses. The financial industry has acknowledged that bitcoin's price performance is second to none—in many ways, bitcoin has become the new global benchmark for investment returns. Over the past decade, gold has doubled, stocks have tripled, but bitcoin has increased 100 times over. In its obliteration of the competition, bitcoin alters our perception of investment and savings. A shift toward a more bitcoin-centric financial system is already underway but remains in its early stages as only 6% of the world has committed to ownership of digital property. By the time bitcoin adoption reaches 2 billion people, a quarter of the world's population, its total market size of $2 trillion today will increase by an order of magnitude, putting *the price of each bitcoin over $1 million*. Let's explain how bitcoin's market size will reach $20 trillion and beyond.

Bitcoin isn't going to replace the dollar anytime soon as the currency of standardized accounting, credit creation, and trade—the dollar is too entrenched in the fibers of the global economy. It will, however, one purchase at a time, continue to replace real estate, cash, and even government bonds as a superior long-term store of value in portfolios around the world. To the dollar's likely persistence, demand for credit won't disappear just because bitcoin now offers an alternative to credit-money: borrowing comes naturally to the economically motivated and is intricately interwoven with the way companies produce goods and services that we consume every day. Companies aren't the only economic participants that depend on borrowing.

People with marketable skills and earning power like to borrow also, qualifying for loans because banks believe they will receive repayment—somebody with a good job or interesting business opportunity can motivate a bank's decision to underwrite a loan, expand its balance sheet, and create deposits from nothing. A married couple that buys a house for their growing family with borrowed funds receives freshly created deposits to do so, credits that come into existence when the loan is underwritten. Imagine, alternatively, that the home's seller only accepted bitcoin as payment—only an entity with existing bitcoin could extend such a loan to the couple, in contrast to a bank that simply *creates* the money. This is an important distinction, because while a bank can facilitate that purchase with money from thin air, a bitcoin-denominated transaction could only take place if one party with bitcoin lends it to the couple—unlike credits, bitcoin cannot be created from nowhere. Both bitcoin and deposits have their place in society and will continue to coexist, as savers want a better money that can't be diluted, and spenders want funds that are easy to borrow.

We don't imagine that bitcoin presents a clear and present threat to the equity asset class. Instead, bitcoin is equity's perfect portfolio complement. Equities, also called stocks or shares, represent an ownership stake in private enterprises and the world's incredible range of production. Bitcoin helps investors save, while equities help them convert those savings into production. For people who hold equity simply as a monetary vehicle, bitcoin *will* compete for those assets, but a large portion of investors hold equity to own productive assets, established profit streams, and the active generation of cash flow.

With this setup, a great financial benefit accrues to bitcoin's long-term holders in the form of declining prices. Bitcoin continually attracts new users to its network due to its widely perceived value as decentralized and scarce digital property, but the increased demand does not and cannot elicit a supply response. The lifeline is open to all—new entrants need not acquire a full coin because each bitcoin is highly divisible. There are 100,000,000 satoshis (named after the creator) in each bitcoin—one satoshi is written as ₿0.00000001. This is similar to how there are 100 cents in each dollar—bitcoin's subunits help it furnish even the tiniest of transactions alongside enormous ones in each block. In real estate investing, buying a fraction of a house isn't possible, but no such barrier exists for small bitcoin transactions.

Now that bitcoin has reached a market value on par with Google, Amazon, and Saudi Aramco, what is the force that will launch it past Microsoft, Apple, and ultimately the world's entire gold stock? In short, *more adoption*—people acquiring and saving in bitcoin instead of choosing traditional investments. We outline the path for bitcoin to increase by at least 10 times over the next 10 years.

The estimated market size of global real estate is well over $300 trillion. How many individuals, families, companies, and countries own land, buildings, and farms as a store of value? It's almost everybody—property is the world's largest asset class. Real estate has perceptible intrinsic value, and common sense helps us see the value of an apartment building that can generate rent, a farm capable of agricultural income, or the land itself increasing in price over time when denominated in credits such as US dollars. Younger generations look at bitcoin as a form of *digital real estate*, but without the costly upkeep and being jurisdictionally tied to the local property title registry. Bitcoin's title registry is a public blockchain, and the cost to maintain bitcoin is zero—no paint chipping, cement cracking, landscape maintenance, or natural disasters to potentially erode the value of the property. Real estate cannot be liquidated at a moment's notice, nor can it easily be subdivided and portioned off. Bitcoin appeals to those who seek scarce property but recognize the advantages of something digital and cryptographic over something physical and government-registered.

Bitcoin also provides an alternative to the world's most popular asset—traditional cash, bank deposits, and money market funds. Unlike banks, bitcoin's market never closes and has a depth that can absorb enormous amounts of capital. An increasing number of cash holders have converted balances to bitcoin, especially if they prefer cash to riskier investments. Across the investment landscape, cash functions as dry powder, a way to describe money that is ready to invest in productive assets. The term originates from how dry gunpowder is necessary for military engagement—wet powder won't ignite and is useless in battle. Investors always prefer a portion of their portfolios be in dry powder so that when an attractive opportunity comes along, they can easily deploy capital instead of freeing it up by forcing a sale of another asset. Bitcoin is the perfect dry powder for investors because it is an asset that can be instantly sold for dollars—in this regard, bitcoin is more appropriately described as a cash position in a portfolio instead of an investment. Compared to a worldwide pool of over $100 trillion in cash assets, bitcoin's $2 trillion market is still miniscule. The digital currency still stands at less than 1% of the combined size of the real estate and global cash markets.

We are not alone in our assessment that bitcoin is a $20 trillion asset. According to a report published in 2022—before bitcoin ETFs, a Digital Fort Knox, and when bitcoin was below $1 trillion in size—the world's third-largest asset manager Fidelity believed bitcoin was heading to a $25 trillion market size and a $1.2 million price per bitcoin as early as 2030. The asset manager's investment thesis centered around bitcoin's role as a store of value in today's increasingly digital world.

Dating back to MIT's Lincoln Labs and BBN, the company that designed the first internet router for ARPANET, the Boston-Cambridge area of Massachusetts had always heavily factored into technology advances in the US. It also hosts Fidelity, an asset manager with over $6 trillion of client funds under management. The company has demonstrated a devotion to bitcoin longer than any other member of the financial industry—CEO Abigail Johnson directed the investment manager's applied technology team to start mining bitcoin in 2014. Fidelity's unorthodox experiment turned heads in financial circles, but that didn't deter its leadership from pressing on.

As the network effects surrounding bitcoin strengthened each time the US advanced the legal standing of digital assets, large investors joined their smaller, retail compatriots in buying bitcoin after seeing legacy players adopting this new asset. Fidelity was not going to miss out, and it was determined to capture the first-mover advantage in the business of bitcoin financial services. It applied for patents for the institutional custody of bitcoin. The cryptographic nature of bitcoin private keys, nodes, mining, and transactions presented a challenge to initiate bitcoin-native services, but Fidelity had the applied technology team to go for it. In 2018, the company launched Fidelity Digital Assets, a custody platform allowing clients to safely keep their bitcoin with a regulated entity that had the technological know-how to store bitcoin on customers' behalf. Fidelity Digital Assets would go on to serve as the custodian to Fidelity's wildly successful bitcoin ETF. Despite being in the ETF business for over two decades, Fidelity's bitcoin ETF astoundingly surpassed every one of its 75 other funds in size in only one year.

The company looks at bitcoin through the lens of technology adoption, comparing it to the internet and smartphones. In its research reports, Fidelity writes that if bitcoin uptake plays out like it did for over 5 billion smartphone users, bitcoin's price will rise to $1.2 million by 2030 and market size to $25 trillion, with over $400 trillion elsewhere in cash and real estate to help us keep Fidelity's prediction in context.[66] The takeaway from Fidelity's comparisons is that we are near the beginning—not the end—of the *Bitcoin Age*. One of its research papers published in 2023 titled "Bitcoin First" explained why the company had dedicated so many resources to bitcoin products, and how bitcoin's monetary network strength derives from two of our three core principles for bitcoin demand—scarcity and decentralization.

Many investors are familiar with the power of network effects, where the value of a given network increases exponentially as the number of its users grows. Monetary networks are no different. However, they are even more powerful than other networks because the incentive to choose the right money is much stronger than any other choice of a network, such as a social network, telephone network, etc. If investors are looking for a digital asset as a monetary good, one with the ability to act as a store of value, then they will naturally choose the one with the largest, most secure, decentralized, and liquid network. Bitcoin as the first truly scarce digital asset ever invented received a first mover advantage and has maintained this advantage over time.[67]

---

66   Jack Neureuter, "Valuing Bitcoin."

67   Chris Kuiper and Jack Neureuter, "Bitcoin First Revisited."

As the price of bitcoin continues to rise and attract new users to this powerful savings technology, the world's understanding of credit-system expansion will increase as a byproduct. Bitcoin purchases themselves are starting to be financed by credit expansion, which amounts to new credit-money purposed to purchase a strictly limited amount of bitcoin. Creditworthy powerhouses such as countries and conglomerates are now beginning their bitcoin journeys, assisted by banks expanding the credit system. Bitcoin's strategic role in the future of geopolitics supports the case for all countries and companies to acquire some, especially with its potential as a neutral measurement of value over a half-century removed from the US dollar's link to gold.

Bitcoin's rise to $2 trillion in market value was mostly driven by the 500 million individuals taking a stake in this new digital property, but its ascent to $20 trillion and beyond will largely be dominated by demand from the largest and oldest institutions in the world. Potentially following the United States into their own strategic bitcoin reserves are Russia, Japan, and Brazil. Nation-states are looking to strengthen their financial and geopolitical positions with bitcoin—entirely dispelling the fears that bitcoin would elicit sweeping restrictions from governments. Much of the world's hesitation to adopt bitcoin stemmed from a fear that governments such as China would ban it, and that such bans would harm the network. There were two major problems with that assumption.

First, a variety of bitcoin bans from the Chinese government have been levied since 2013, but none of them materially impacted the trajectory of the network. China's sweeping mining ban in 2021 did cause a significant drop in bitcoin's mining difficulty, but the network quickly recovered after only four months. Chinese equipment was sold off to miners from Texas to Kazakhstan, who eventually brought those machines back online. Second, China has already banned most of the open internet within its borders without affecting global internet adoption—so we should expect a similar trajectory for bitcoin as an internet protocol. Bitcoin's open monetary network cannot be stopped by any single nation, no matter how powerful, and the absence of Chinese adoption has had no negative impact on bitcoin's value. With strategic reserves being implemented across the free world, nation-states are gravitating toward bitcoin for survival—the voices of 500 million people are too loud to ignore, and policymakers in many representative governments are responding. Bitcoin isn't evolving as a currency for buying a cup of coffee but as the world's only form of digital real estate, currently up for grabs at undervalued market prices.

* * *

Keeping bitcoin sufficiently decentralized requires different actors to compete over block rewards so that no single entity can control which transactions make it into the bitcoin blockchain. Miners consume energy to engage in this competition, and copious amounts of it. Machines perform quintillions of hashes per second across the network to try and generate a valid bitcoin block. This requires as much electricity as a medium-sized nation does, but still much less than what is consumed by the global financial industry. Bank branches, office headquarters, ATM machines, data centers, cooling the data centers, payment processing devices, and business travel combine to require far more energy than bitcoin mining. Nevertheless, bitcoin's energy consumption has been maligned over its young history.

Thankfully, those tides are turning as an important truth is slowly revealed. Because bitcoin mining requires blistering amounts of energy consumption, miners are looking for the cheapest possible power. Oil rarely falls into that category—it is dense, transportable, and more expensive than renewable sources, which are significantly more cost-effective. As a sector, bitcoin mining has one of the highest rates of renewable energy consumption in the world. Now, it flocks to where power is cheapest and often non-transportable, usually next to a hydroelectric facility. In Africa, bitcoin miners are entering mutually beneficial relationships with remote villages to build small hydroelectric dams, share the electricity with the locals, and profit from block generation.

Another inspiring byproduct of bitcoin mining gravitating toward the cheapest forms of energy is the mitigation of methane emissions. Statistics show that an unacceptable 40% of all global waste goes into open-pit landfills—as the trash decays, harmful methane emissions poison the breathing air of anybody living within a few miles, causing respiratory illnesses in millions of people, with over 75% of these open-pit landfills residing in Asia and Africa. Bitcoin miners have devised a creative solution—capture and collect the methane and burn it to power generators that mine bitcoin. Once the methane is burned, it's far less harmful to humans, leading to another win-win situation in which communities breathe cleaner air, bitcoin miners can profit, and the network grows more secure as difficulty rises. We are doubtful that Satoshi Nakamoto designed bitcoin with an ambition to improve air quality and waste management, but bitcoin is changing the world in ways he, or even we, could never have imagined.

When energy producers drill for oil, associated natural gas can escape during the process. Usually, there is no feasible way for the oil drillers to capture this gas by storage or pipeline, so in order to get rid of it without releasing it directly into the environment, producers simply burn it. This process of gas flaring is extremely common around the world, but in the same way that bitcoin miners are burning methane extracted from landfills for power generation, they are capturing natural gas that would otherwise be flared and using it as fuel. The world's largest oil companies, including ExxonMobil and Shell, have already started mining bitcoin to utilize natural gas that would otherwise be wasted, showing us just how far the global bitcoin mining industry has come from the early days of being able to generate blocks on an average home computer.

Stranded energy describes excess hydroelectric power that isn't immediately consumed or solar power that cannot be stored due to lacking battery infrastructure and power loss when electricity is transmitted over long distances. It's the perfect fuel for electricity-powered bitcoin miners—the largest power utility in Japan, TEPCO, is mining bitcoin with excess solar and wind power that would otherwise have been wasted. Bitcoin mining can alter the way we produce and consume energy as a society because it monetizes electricity anywhere it can be produced. Above all, the energy required to support the bitcoin network is justified by every individual user whose life is better off thanks to this freedom-oriented savings technology.

* * *

Bitcoin's blockchain architecture, in which every node in the network must keep a slow enough pace to maintain coordination, doesn't necessarily facilitate instant commerce. In the same post about high-powered money from 2010, Hal Finney described why bitcoin wouldn't exist alone—it would require a second-layer protocol to help move it more quickly over the internet:

> *Bitcoin itself cannot scale to have every single financial transaction in the world be broadcast to everyone and included in the block chain. There needs to be a secondary level of payment systems which is lighter weight and more efficient.[68]*

---

68 *Finney, "Bitcoin Bank."*

His prediction came true in 2017 with the Lightning Network, a protocol that leverages bitcoin's blockchain to bring *instant settlement* to bitcoin. Joining the Lightning Network requires an escrow of funds and connectivity to payment routers, utilizing a web of bitcoin users to transfer funds from point A to point B. Bitcoin wallet provider Breez recently produced a study showing that 650 million people around the world now have access to bitcoin transactions powered by Lightning. This second-layer protocol makes micropayments over the internet possible—with instant bitcoin transactions as low as ฿0.00000001 not only feasible but functioning perfectly. With bitcoin's "lighter weight" payment protocol now fully operational, bitcoin works as both a store of value and a medium of exchange—a joint study between Fidelity and bitcoin infrastructure company Voltage determined that over Lightning, transactions ฿0.01 or less complete in under one second.[69]

* * *

Bitcoin's milestones over the course of its brief 16-year history have confounded many. There are people who believe the credit system doesn't need fixing, those who will tell you not to trust the magic internet money, and many who simply do not yet understand what drives bitcoin's demand. But try as they might, it is hard to deny that a *Bitcoin Age* of freedom,

---

69 Daniel Gray, "Lightning Network."

empowerment, and peaceful economic interaction is just beginning. In addition to the obvious benefits from a world of falling prices, bitcoin could bring us the gift of *positive societal change.* It has the potential to drive a reassessment of our global borrowing patterns and force banks to adapt to a future without dollars as the only global reserve currency. As bitcoin flies around the internet without the use of the dollar, banks, a central server, hidden treasure, or Jedi mind tricks, we are presented with a once-in-a-generation opportunity to rethink money. Let us not squander this most fortunate discovery.

ACKNOWLEDGEMENTS

WRITING A BOOK IS A DEEPLY PERSONAL JOURNEY, BUT AT the same time, it is a family effort. To my wife Chandni and our daughter Ria, thank you both for supporting me all the way. Chandni, I could not have done any of this without all your encouragement, quiet side-by-side reading and writing, and love. Thank you for an amazing life of friendship and partnership. Ria, you are our treasure. We can't wait to continue exploring the globe together, but most of all, just being a family.

To my parents and Chandni's parents—thank you for your guidance and prayers throughout. Jay, Kashvi, & Jashan, Archana, Dhruv, & Naina—I love you all.

The Bitcoin Layer team—it is hard to describe my gratitude. Building this company with you all is epic. Joe Consorti, Matthew Ball, Jordan Williams, Augustine Carrasco, and Demian Schatt—thank you.

Many people helped me in the writing of this book, offering support, editing, teaching, coaching, and just being there. Matt Snow, Joakim Book, Vikram Amritraj, Prakash Amritraj, Stephen Amritraj, Justin Anderson, Matt Malcom, Michael Howell, Jeff Booth, Pierre Rochard, my USC students, and subscribers to The Bitcoin Layer—thank you. Readers of *Layered Money*—you all are part of this second book. Thank you to Anton Khodakovsky for another brilliant cover.

US National Median House Price

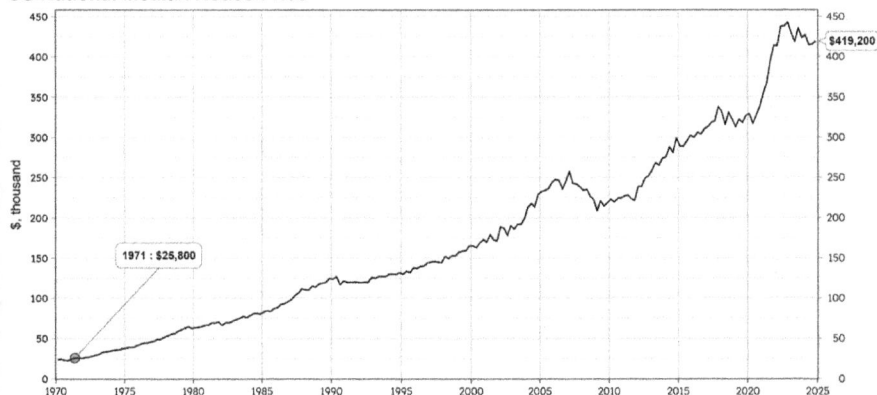

Source: The Bitcoin Layer, United States Census Bureau, Macrobond

US Median Household Income

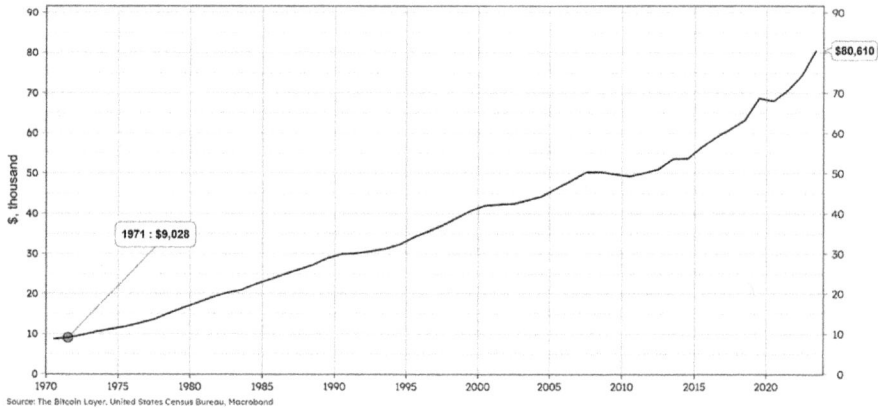

1971 : $9,028

$80,610

$, thousand

Source: The Bitcoin Layer, United States Census Bureau, Macrobond

US House Price to Income Ratio

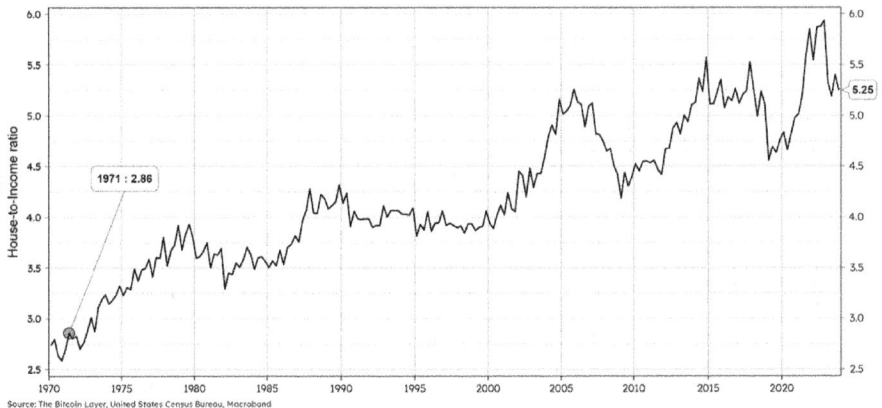

US House Price to Income Ratio

1971 : 2.86

5.25

Source: The Bitcoin Layer, United States Census Bureau, Macroband

US National Median House Price in Bitcoin

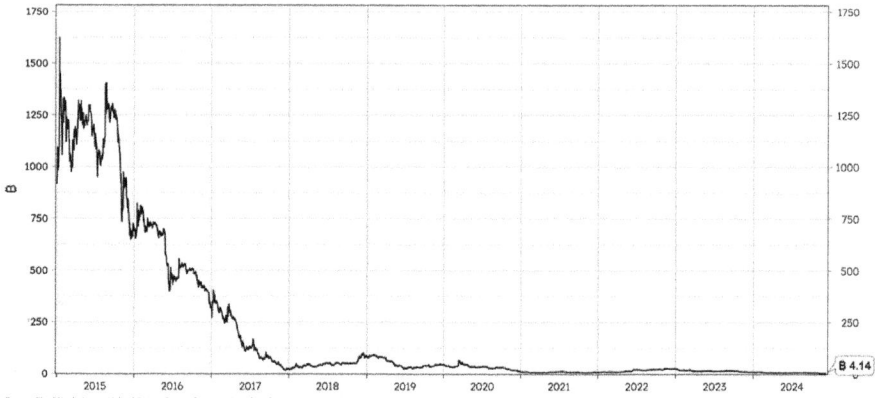

Source: The Bitcoin Layer, United States Census Bureau, Macrobond

US National Median House Price in Bitcoin (logarithmic)

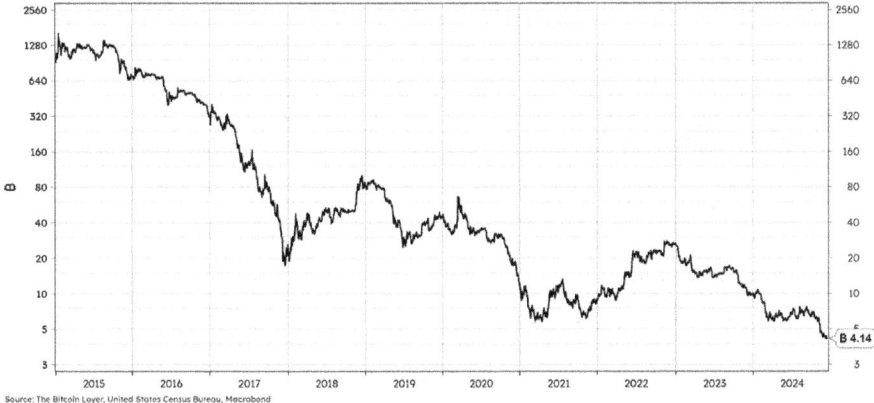

Source: The Bitcoin Layer, United States Census Bureau, Macrobond

Bitcoin Price

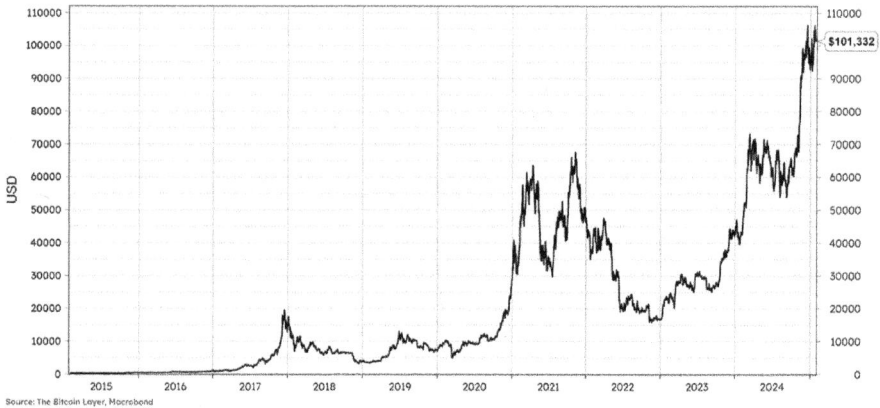

$101,332

Source: The Bitcoin Layer, Macrobond

Bitcoin Price (logarithmic)

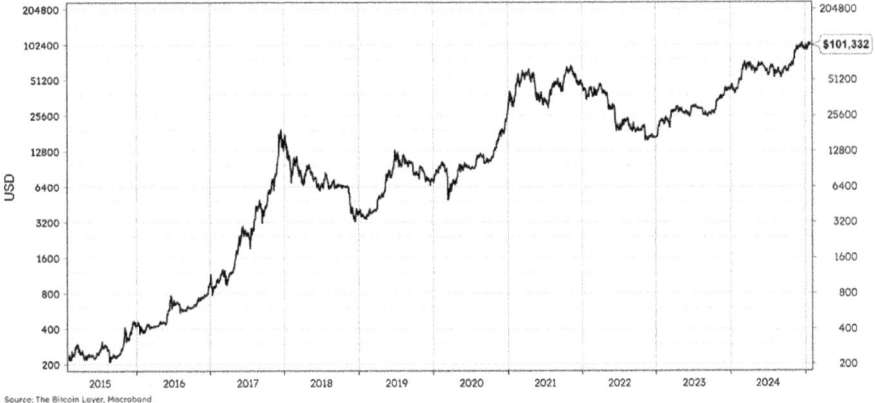

Source: The Bitcoin Layer, Macrobond

Altamura, Carlo Edoardo. "The Paradox of the 1970s: The Renaissance of International Banking and the Rise of Public Debt," *Journal of Modern European History*, 15, 4, 2017: 529–553.

Booth, Jeff. *Price of Tomorrow: Why Deflation is the Key to an Abundant Future*. Stanley Press, 2020.

Burn, Gary. "The State, the City and the Euromarkets," *Review of International Political Economy*, vol. 6, 2, 1999: 225–261.

Cagan, Philip. "High-Powered Money," in *Determinants and Effects of Changes in the Stock of Money, 1875–1960*, NBER, January 1965.

Cerf, Vinton G. "Oral-History," 26 January 2021. Available online via Engineering and Technology History Wiki: https://ethw.org/Oral-History:Vinton_Cerf

Cerf, Vinton G. "Paul Baran 1926-2011," National Academy of Engineering. https://www.nae.edu/189753/PAUL-BARAN-19262011

CIA. "The Asia-Dollar Market," Intelligence Memorandum. ER IM
70-74, June 1970. Available online via: https://www.cia.gov/read-
ingroom/docs/CIA-RDP85T00875R001600030074-7.pdf

Citigroup. "1902: IBC Pioneers Trade Finance in Asia." Available
online via: https://www.citigroup.com/global/about-us/
heritage/1902/ibc-pioneers-trade-finance-in-asia

CME Group. "CME Group and Crypto Facilities Announce Launch
of Bitcoin Reference Rate and Real-Time Index," 2 May
2016. Available online via: https://investor.cmegroup.com/
static-files/27d678e1-a9fe-4720-8fdb-e504300d28d8

Diffie, Whitfield and Hellman, Martin. "New Directions in
Cryptography," *IEEE Transactions on Information Theory*, vol
IT-22, 6 November 1976: 644–654.

FinCEN, "Guidance: FIN-2013-G001," Department of the Treasury
Financial Crimes Enforcement Network, 18 March 2013: https://
www.fincen.gov/statutes_regs/guidance/pdf/FIN-2013-G001.pdf

Finney, Hal. "Bitcoin v0.1 released," 11 January 2009. Available via
Satoshi Nakamoto Institute: https://satoshi.nakamotoinstitute.
org/emails/bitcoin-list/threads/4/#21312757

Finney, Hal. "Re: Bitcoin and the Efficient Market Hypothesis,"
BitcoinTalk.org, 4 June 2011: https://bitcointalk.org/index.
php?topic=11765.msg169026#msg169026

Finney, Hal. "Re: Bitcoin Bank," *BitcoinTalk.org*, 30 December 2010: https://bitcointalk.org/index.php?topic=2500. msg34211#msg34211

Finney, Hal. "Why Remailers…" Cypherpunks mailing list, 15 November 1992: https://cypherpunks.venona.com/date/1992/11/ msg00108.html#:~:text=The%20computer%20can%20be%20 used%20as%20a%20tool%20to%0Aliberate%20and%20pro- tect%20people%2C%20rather%20than%20to%20control%20 them

Friedrich, Klaus. "The Euro-Dollar System and International Liquidity," *Journal of Money, Credit and Banking*, 2, 3, Aug., 1970: 337–347.

Gray, Daniel. "The Lightning Network: Expanding Bitcoin Use Cases—Moving Beyond One-to-One Payments," Research Study, Fidelity Digital Assets, 19 February 2025: https:// www.fidelitydigitalassets.com/research-and-insights/ lightning-network-expanding-bitcoin-use-cases

Green, Jeremy. "Anglo-American Development, the Euromarkets, and the Deeper Origins of Neoliberal Deregulation," *Review of International Studies*, 42, 3, 2016: 425–449.

Griffin, G. Edward. *The Creature from Jekyll Island: A Second Look at the Federal Reserve*. Dauphin Publications, 2010.

Haber, Stuart and Stornetta, Scott. "How To Time-Stamp a Digital Document," *Journal of Cryptology*, 3: 1991: 99–111.

Hafner, Katie and Lyon, Matthew. *Where Wizards Stay Up Late: The Origins of the Internet*. New York: Simon & Schuster, 1996.

Holmes, Alan R., and Klopstock, Fred H. "The Market for Dollar Deposits in Europe," Federal Reserve Bank of New York Monthly Review, November 1960: 197–202.

Hughes, Eric. "A Cypherpunk's Manifesto," 9 March 1993. Available via Satoshi Nakamoto Institute: https://cdn.nakamotoinstitute. org/docs/cypherpunk-manifesto.txt

Isaacson, Walter. *The Innovators: How a Group of Hackers, Geniuses, and Geeks Created the Digital Revolution*. New York: Simon & Schuster, 2014.

Kaufman, Henry. *Interest Rates, the Markets, and the New Financial World*. New York: Crown, 1986.

kencausey. "Re: Overflow bug SERIOUS," 15 August 2010. Available via Satoshi Nakamoto Institute: https://satoshi.nakamotoinstitute. org/posts/bitcointalk/threads/185/#8

Kim, Seung Woo. "Knowledge, Contestation and Authority in the Eurodollar Market, 1959–64," in *Money and Markets: Essays in Honour of Martin Daunton*, edited by Julian Hoppit, Duncan

Needham, and Adrian Leonard, 145–160. Martlesham: Boydell & Brewer, 2019.

Klopstock, Fred H. "The International Money Market: Structure, Scope and Instruments," *The Journal of Finance*, vol 2, 2, Papers and Proceedings of the Twenty-Third Annual Meeting of the American Finance Association, Chicago, IL December 28-30, 1964. May 1965: 182–208.

Kuiper, Chris and Neureuter, Jack. "Bitcoin First Revisited: Why Investors Need to Consider Bitcoin Separately from Other Digital Assets," Fidelity Digital Assets, September 2023. Available online via: https://www.fidelitydigitalassets.com/sites/g/files/ djuvja3256/files/acquiadam/1012662.6.0%20-%20FDAS%20 Bitcoin%20First%20Revisited%20V1.pdf

Leimone, John E. "The Euro-Dollar Market: An Element in Monetary Policy," Federal Reserve Bank of Atlanta Monthly Review, 53, 8, 1968: 102–109.

Levy, Steven. *Crypto: How the Code Rebels Beat the Government Saving Privacy in the Digital Age*. New York: Viking Press, 2001.

Licklider, J.C.R. "Man-Computer Symbiosis," *IRE Transactions on Human Factors in Electronics* vol. HFE-1, March 1960: 4–11. Available via: https://groups.csail.mit.edu/medg/people/psz/ Licklider.html

Menand, Lev. "Lots More with lev Menand on the Eurodollar Market Now," *Odd Lots* podcast with Tracy Alloway and Joe Weisenthal, *Bloomberg* 17 January 2025: https://www.bloomberg.com/news/articles/2025-01-17/lots-more-with-lev-menand-on-the-eurodollar-market-now

Nakamoto, Satoshi. "Bitcoin Open Source Implementation of P2P Currency," 11 February 2009. Available via Satoshi Nakamoto Institute: https://satoshi.nakamotoinstitute.org/posts/p2pfoundation/1/

Nakamoto, Satoshi. "Bitcoin Open Source Implementation of P2P Currency," 18 February 2009. Available via Satoshi Nakamoto Institute: https://satoshi.nakamotoinstitute.org/posts/p2pfoundation/3/

Nakamoto, Satoshi. "Bitcoin P2P e-Cash Paper," 31 October–17 November 2008. Available via Satoshi Nakamoto Institute: https://satoshi.nakamotoinstitute.org/emails/cryptography/threads/1/

Nakamoto, Satoshi. "Bitcoin v0.1 Released," 16 January 2009. Available via Satoshi Nakamoto Institute: https://satoshi.nakamotoinstitute.org/emails/cryptography/17/

Nakamoto, Satoshi. "Bitcoin v0.1 Released," 8 January 2009. Available via Satoshi Nakamoto Institute: https://satoshi.nakamotoinstitute.org/emails/cryptography/16/

Nakamoto, Satoshi. "Bitcoin: A Peer-to-Peer Electronic Cash System,"
31 October 2008. Available via Satoshi Nakamoto Institute:
https://cdn.nakamotoinstitute.org/docs/bitcoin.pdf

Nakamoto, Satoshi. "Re: PC World Article on Bitcoin," 11 December
2010. Available via Satoshi Nakamoto Institute: https://satoshi.
nakamotoinstitute.org/posts/bitcointalk/542/

Namcios. "Bitcoin Pizza Day: P2P Digital Cash
Actualized 12 Years Ago," *Bitcoin Magazine,* 22
May 2022: https://bitcoinmagazine.com/culture/
bitcoin-pizza-day-p2p-digital-cash-actualized-12-years-ago

National Park Service. "The Transcontinental Telegraph," 7 May 2024.
Available online via: https://www.nps.gov/articles/000/the-trans-
continental-telegraph.htm

Neureuter, Jack. "Valuing Bitcoin," Fidelity Digital Assets, June
2022. Available online via: https://www.fidelitydigitalassets.
com/sites/g/files/djuvja3256/files/acquiadam/1145306.1.0%20
-%20Fidelity%20Digital%20Assets%20Valuing%20Bitcoin%20
%2805.07%29.pdf

Rauterberg, Gabriel and Younger, Joshua. "The Hidden Monetary
State," *Arizona State Law Journal,* 56, 2024: 987–1074: https://
arizonastatelawjournal.org/wp-content/uploads/2024/08/
Rauterberg_PUB.pdf

Raz, Guy. "'Lo' and Behold: A Communication Revolution," *NPR*, 29 October 2009: https://www.npr.org/2009/10/29/114280698/lo-and-behold-a-communication-revolution

Rizzo, Pete. "Read Adam Back's Complete Emails with Bitcoin Creator Satoshi Nakamoto," *Bitcoin Magazine*, 23 February 2024: https://bitcoinmagazine.com/technical/bitcoin-adam-backs-complete-emails-satoshi-nakamoto

Russell, Andrew L. *Open Standards and the Digital Age: History, Ideology, and Networks*. New York: Cambridge University Press, 2014.

Schenk, Catherine. "The Origins of the Eurodollar Market in London: 1955-1963," *Explorations in Economic History*, 35, 1998: 221–238.

Siemens. "Halfway Around the World in 28 Minutes: Building the Indo-European Telegraph Line 150 Years Ago." Available online via: https://www.siemens.com/global/en/company/about/history/stories/indo-european-telegraph-line.html

Stevens, Hallam. "Hans Peter Luhn and the Birth of the Hashing Algorithm," *IEEE Spectrum*, 30 Jan 2018. Available online via: https://spectrum.ieee.org/hans-peter-luhn-and-the-birth-of-the-hashing-algorithm

Time Magazine. "Money: De Gaulle v. the Dollar," *Time*, 12 February 1965: https://time.com/archive/6634666/money-de-gaulle-v-the-dollar/

Toniolo, Gianni. *Central Bank Cooperation at the Bank for International Settlements, 1930–1973*. New York: Cambridge University Press, 2005.

van Wirdum, Aaron. *The Genesis Book: The Story of the People and Projects That Inspired Bitcoin*. Nashville, TN.: Bitcoin Magazine Books, 2024.

Wheeler, Tom. *From Gutenberg to Google: The History of Our Future*. Lanham, MD: Rowman & Littlefield Publishers: 2019.

White House. "Establishment of the Strategic Bitcoin Reserve and United States Digital Asset Stockpile," Executive Order 14233, 06 Mar 2025. Available online via: https://www.whitehouse.gov/presidential-actions/2025/03/establishment-of-the-strategic-bitcoin-reserveand-united-states-digital-asset-stockpile/

White House. "Strengthening American Leadership in Digital Financial Technology," Executive Order 14178, 23 Jan 2025. Available online via: https://www.whitehouse.gov/presidential-actions/2025/01/strengthening-american-leadership-in-digital-financial-technology/

Younger, Josh. "Josh Younger on the Origin Story of the Shadow Banking System," *Odd Lots* podcast with Tracy Alloway and Joe Weisenthal, *Bloomberg*, 7 November 2022: https://www.youtube.com/watch?v=edpbYZV_61s&ab_channel=BloombergPodcasts

Younger, Josh. "Josh Younger on the Surprising Origins of Eurodollars and Petrodollars," *Odd Lots* podcast with Tracy Alloway and Joe Weisenthal, *Bloomberg*, 19 June 2023: https://www.bloomberg.com/news/articles/2023-06-19/josh-younger-on-the-origins-of-eurodollars-and-petrodollars

Zimmermann, Philip. "Why I Wrote PGP," Philzimmermann.com, 1991 [1999]: https://www.philzimmermann.com/EN/essays/WhyIWrotePGP.html

Zweig, Phillip L., *Wriston: Walter Wriston, Citibank, and the Rise and Fall of American Financial Supremacy*. New York: Crown Publishers, 2005.

ABOUT THE AUTHOR

NIK BHATIA is founder of The Bitcoin Layer, a bitcoin and global macro research firm, and author of the best-selling book *Layered Money*. He is a CFA charterholder, former US Treasuries and money markets trader, and teaches fixed income and bitcoin as a professor at the USC Marshall School of Business.

THEBITCOINLAYER.COM

www.ingramcontent.com/pod-product-compliance
Lightning Source LLC
Chambersburg PA
CBHW042139210326
41458CB00085B/6837/J